"If you never want to be criticized, for goodness' sake don't do anything new."
–Jeff Bezos

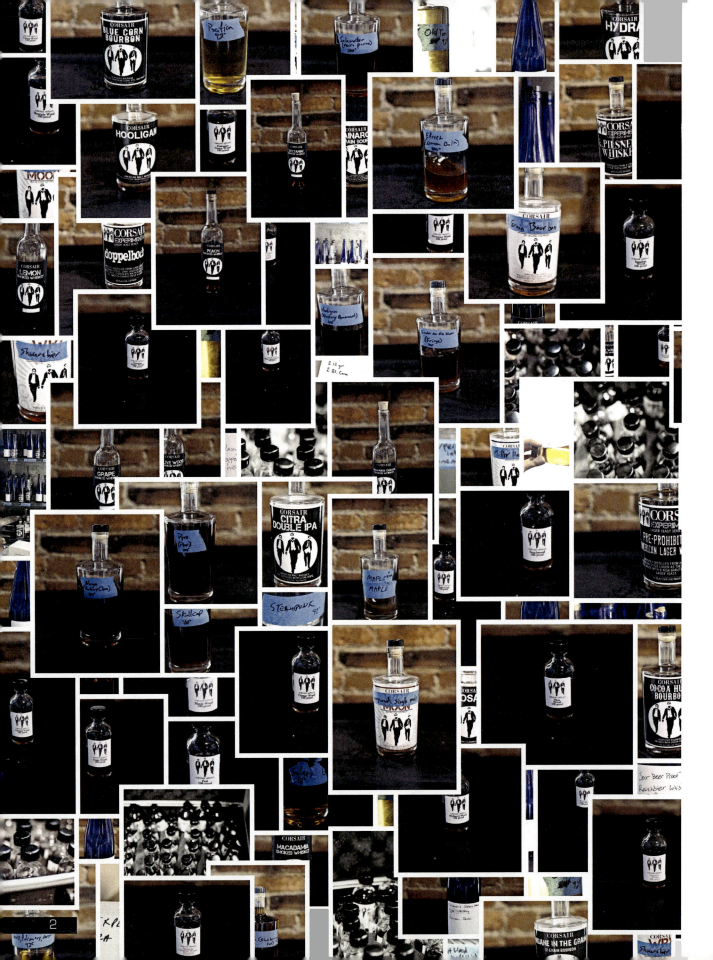

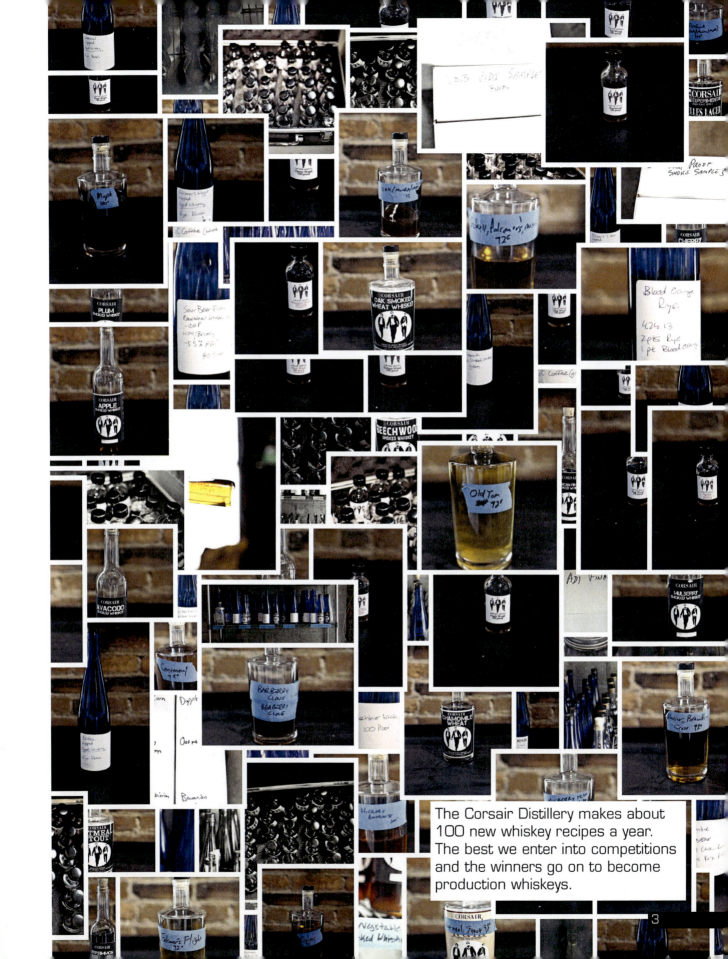

The Corsair Distillery makes about 100 new whiskey recipes a year. The best we enter into competitions and the winners go on to become production whiskeys.

FIRE WATER

EXPERIMENTAL SMOKED MALTS AND WHISKEYS

by Darek Bell, Owner of the Corsair Distillery

© 2013 by Darek Bell

All rights reserved—no part of this book may be reproduced in any form without permission in writing from the author. All images in this book have been reproduced with the knowledge and prior consent of the artists concerned, and no responsibility is accepted by producer, publisher, or printer for any infringement of copyright or otherwise, arising from the contents of this publication. Every effort has been made to ensure that credits comply with information supplied. We apologize for any inaccuracies that may have ocurred and will resolve any inaccurate or missing information in a subsequent publishing of this book.

ISBN: 978-0-9833500-1-9

Edited by Amy Lee Bell

Copy Editing by Matt Strickland and Nicki Wood

Photography by Anthony Matula

Cover imagery by Pete Rodman and Anthony Matula

Foreward by Clay Risen

Nosings by Nancy Fraley and Julia Nourney

Cocktail recipes by Charles Christian Fields

Back cover photo of author by Greg Miller

Additional Photographs by Andrea Behrends, Dani Atkins, Pete Rodman, Kerry Woo, Darek Bell, Clay Smith, Becca Smith, and Andrew Webber

THIS BOOK IS DEDICATED

first of all to Amy Lee Bell, my beautiful wife and partner in crime,

and to Andrew Webber, my oldest friend and fellow gentleman pirate,

and to all the talented distillers and brewers I get to work with at the Corsair Artisan Distillery: Matt Strickland, Andrea Clodfelter, Jason Ingram, Tyler Crowell, Will Atkinson, Clay Smith, Aaron Marcum, Erik Rothfuss, Emily Kendall, Nick Hansen, Austin Reese, Alex England, Morgan Maxwell, Lex Reeves, Colton Weinstein, Steve Whitledge, Jacob Bansmer, Jason Zeno, Stuart Chescheir, Marissa Korthuis, Sean Jewett, Elissa McIntyre, Ben Kickert, Jay Settle, Deb Parrish, and Matthew Webber. I also want to thank David Pickerall and Bill Owens for their infinite wisdom. I have to thank Anthony Matula for his infinite patience. Clay Risen, Lew Bryson, Dave Broom, Chris Chamberlain, and Dominic Roskrow have also given me invaluable advice. I have some important business mentors I need to thank: Clayton McWhorter, Michael Burcham, Keith Pyle, Jody Evans, Robert Davidson, Jeff Hopmeyer, Don Brain, and Stuart McWhorter. Finally, I had some wonderful allies that helped us open the Tennessee distillery: Toby Compton, Greg Hinote, Mayor Karl Dean, Doug Sloan, Councilman Erica Gilmore, Senator Bill Ketron, Micki Yearwood, and big thanks to Mike Williams.

Finally I want to dedicate this to my parents, Sharon and Ray Bell (1941-2010), and my brother Brad.

FIRE WATER

EXPERIMENTAL SMOKED MALT AND WHISKEYS
by Darek Bell, Owner of the Corsair Distillery

Nosings by Nancy Fraley and Julia Nourney

80 different smoked fuel sources are explored for making dynamic smoked malt and whiskeys...without peat.

Darek Bell is the owner of the Corsair Distillery. He started Corsair with his wife Amy Lee Bell, and childhood best friend Andrew Webber in 2008. Darek's innovative and adventurous spirits have won 92 medals at international spirits competitions. His whiskeys have been praised in publications like The New York Times, Food and Wine, Saveur, Imbibe, Whisky Magazine, Time Out New York, and Maxim.com. Darek was trained at the Siebel Brewing Institute and is a graduate of the Bruichladdich Distilling Academy in Islay, Scotland. One of his smoked whiskey recipes, Triple Smoke, was named "Artisan Whiskey of the Year" by Whisky Advocate Magazine.

CORSAIR'S PHILOSOPHY

If it has been done before we are not interested in doing it.

Imitation is suicide.

Creativity is free.

Innovate or die.

Our goal is to make whiskeys the world has never seen before.

ACKNOWLEDGEMENTS

This book would not be possible without the support of my awesome wife-ninja: Amy Lee Bell. She inspires me to be true to my self, make kick-ass booze, protect small furry animals whenever possible, and be a better man. I also have to thank a couple of awesome mentors out there who have done so much to make me a better brewer, distiller, experimenter, whatever-er: Bill Owens at ADI. Duncan McGillivray and Jim McEwan at Bruichladdich, Jeff Hopmeyer, and Dave Pickerall.

DISCLAIMER

Please don't do something stupid and kill yourself. Distilling can be dangerous. High proof spirits are very flammable. It is easy to burn yourself. Dust from grains can be quite flammable. If you look at the history of extinct malting facilities, many of them were by fires. Smoking grain is dangerous on many levels. Barrels are heavy and great for crushing small toes. I wrote this book hoping people would smoke barley, not set their house on fire.

LEGALITIES

Unfortunately, only a few countries in the world allow legal home distilling. New Zealand, for example, is one of them. In the United States, distilling without a federal permit is a felony. This is no parking ticket. It is life destroying: five years in jail and a $10,000 fine, boys and girls. People often think you can make moonshine at home for personal use only. Wrong, it is illegal. Period.

Making spirits without a license is illegal. Period.

There is an interesting work-around. The alternative energy movement opened up an exciting possibility. You can get a legal "fuel ethanol permit" from the federal government. You are only allowed to make alcohol to be used for fuel. You are not allowed to drink it. However this is still a great and legal avenue to learn distilling. Why these laws? The government gets a lot of taxes from alcoholic beverages. They need the money right now. Strangely, this is extremely shortsighted on the government's part. In New Zealand, alcohol tax collections went up after home distilling was legalized, as people went out to try lots of different brands in order to educate themselves. Although you are not supposed to make whiskey with it, if you did get busted, having a fuel ethanol permit would be much, much better than having nothing at all. I am in no way condoning anything illegal. If someone wants to create their own whiskey, they need to 1) move to New Zealand, 2) start a craft distillery legally, 3) get a legal fuel ethanol permit, or 4) make it illegally knowing full well the ramifications if you get busted.

One more thing. Some wood species are endangered and protected. Please do not use these woods. The CITES international list can tell you what is protected: www.cites.org/eng/resources/species.html

Do not use endangered woods.

So who is this book for? Whiskey geeks like myself who are fascinated about all things whiskey and who are just curious about this whole craft distilling movement. Fuel ethanol enthusiasts will be excited by some of the alternative grains and the chapter on building your own still. Entrepreneurs trying to launch their own craft distillery will get a lot out of every chapter. Underground moonshiners looking to hone their craft will get a lot out of it. I hope one day home distilling is legal like home brewing and home winemaking in North America. There were people sternly against legalizing home brewing of beer. Forty years later the earth did not collide with the sun. The world did not end. Western civilization did not become so debauched it destroyed itself. Sounds a bit like the rhetoric before prohibition? And how did that turn out again? Oh yeah, prohibition was a catastrophic failure that created organized crime and violence far worse than the drinking it did not actually stop. For the moment, home distilling is illegal. I hope one day it is legalized, probably long after my time. When it finally becomes legal, I hope people will be inspired to try many of the recipes in this book. Finally, I wish that entrepreneurs looking to launch new craft distilleries will use this book to expand the horizons of what we think of as whiskey, and make smoked whiskey.

Happy distilling.

Darek

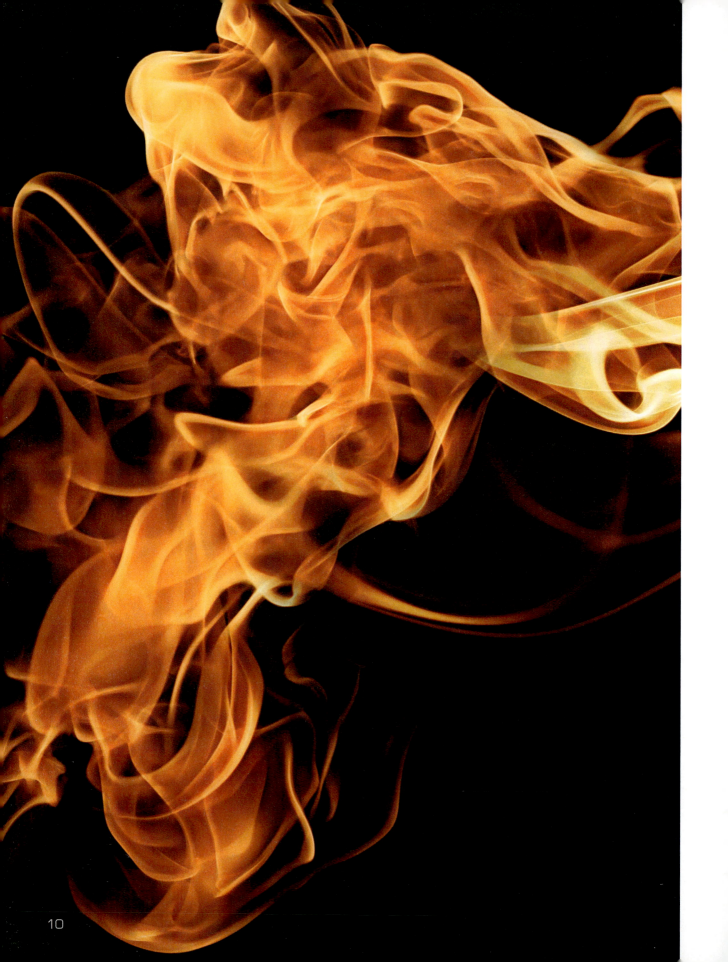

FIRE WATER

CONTENTS

Contents

Foreward by Clay Risen	14
Preface	16
Why Smoked Whiskeys	18
Malting	25
Smoking techniques	35
Smoking woods	62
Smoking barrels	107
Barks/roots	112
Smoking herbs	126
Blending	156
Smoky cocktails	172
So what's the best?	182
Index, credits	191

CONTENTS

Fuel Sources

WOODS

ALDER WOOD	66	MANZANITA WOOD	91
ALMOND WOOD	67	MAPLE WOOD	92
APPLE WOOD	68	MESQUITE WOOD	93
APRICOT WOOD	69	MULBERRY WOOD	94
ASH WOOD	70	OREGON MYRTLE WOOD	95
AVOCADO WOOD	71	NECTARINE WOOD	96
BEECH WOOD	73	OLIVE WOOD	97
BIRCH WOOD	73	ORANGE WOOD	98
BLACK WALNUT WOOD	75	PEACH WOOD	99
CEDAR WOOD	76	PEAR WOOD	100
CHERRY WOOD	77	PECAN WOOD	101
COFFEE WOOD	78	PERSIMMON WOOD	102
COTTONWOOD	79	PLUM WOOD	103
CRABAPPLE	80	RED OAK WOOD	104
GRAPE WOOD	81	SASSAFRAS WOOD	105
HAWAIIAN GUAVA	82	WHITE OAK WOOD	106
HAWAIIAN KIAWE	83		
HAWAIIAN OHIA	84		

BARRELS

HICKORY WOOD	85	BOURBON BARREL	108
JAMAICAN PIMENTO	86	CABERNET BARREL	109
LEMON WOOD	87	FRENCH OAK BARREL	110
LILAC WOOD	88	TABASCO® BARREL	111
MACADAMIA WOOD	89		
MANUKA WOOD	90		

CONTENTS

BARKS/ROOTS

BAYBERRY ROOT	113	MINT	139
BIRCH BARK	114	MUGWORT	142
BLACKBERRY ROOT	115	MULLEIN LEAF	143
BUTTERNUT BARK	116	OSHA	144
CASCARA BARK	117	PEPPERMINT	145
CATUABA BARK	118	SAGE	147
FRINGE TREE BARK	119	SKULLCAP	148
JAMAICAN DOGWOOD	120	SPEARMINT	149
MUIRA PUAMA BARK	121	JUNIPER	150
PRICKLY ASH BARK	122	TARRAGON	151
QUASSIA BARK	123	VIOLET	153
WHITE WILLOW BARK	124	WORMWOOD	155
YOHIMBE BARK	125		

HERBS

ANGELICA	128
ANISE	129
CALAMUS ROOT	130
CATNIP	131
CLOVE	132
GINGER	133
JASMINE	134
LAVENDER	135
LEMON BALM	137
LICORICE	138

FOREWARD

Like many things – popular music, the steam engine, democracy – whiskey was invented in Europe and revolutionized in America. We do things differently here, going back to the time when Scots-Irish and German settlers on the post-independence frontier decided to use corn, rather than just rye or barley, in their whiskey mash.

Corn whiskey, and bourbon in particular, took hold quickly, and became the national tipple for much of the 19th and 20th centuries. But by the latter half of the latter century American whiskey lay in a fallow field. Here I am referring to the "white years," the period from roughly 1970 to 2000 when baby boomers rebelled against the brown spirits of their forefathers and sipped on white wine, unaged rum and vodka.

The whites still dominate the market. But whiskey, and especially American ryes and bourbons, is making a rapid comeback, thanks to a counter-revolt by the boomers' millennial offspring. At first, the turn, or return, to brown spirits benefited the "legacy" styles and those craft distillers who focused on cloning those styles. But that is starting to change, and the book currently in your hands (or on your handheld device of choice) points to some of the exciting directions the whiskey business may be headed.

Often times craft distillers will compare themselves to the craft brewers of the 1980s and 1990s, who first began offering an alternative to the big, bland brews of Miller, Coors and Co. The problem, as clever consumers were quick to point out, is that while Miller Lite may bear only a passing resemblance to beer, the average whiskey coming out of Heaven Hill, Jim Beam, or Buffalo Trace is quite good – and at a price point that craft distillers couldn't dream of meeting.

All of which means that the quicker the next phase in the craft whiskey movement arrives, the better. And that is where Darek Bell comes in. With "Fire Water" and his previous book "Alt Whiskeys," Bell has mapped in intricate detail everything that American craft whiskey can be – must be, in fact, if it is to carve out a place for itself alongside the Elijah Craigs and Elmer T. Lee's of the world.

In some ways this second iteration in the craft whiskey evolution is a better analog to craft beer's life story than the first. By the 1990s, craft brewers had mastered the basics of their art – and were ready, like good Americans, to shake things up. And so was born the Cascadian Dark Ale, the Russian Imperial Stout, the Imperial Pale Ale – variations on old themes, but amped up, twisted, changed on a fundamental level. Innovators like Sam Calagione of Dogfish Head and Doug and Wynne Odell of Odell Brewing took old-world styles and refashioned them, adding new ingredients and fiddling with the brewing process to make something different.

We can see the same thing just beginning to happen with craft distilling – and nowhere more so than at Nashville's Corsair Artisan Distilling, where Bell hangs his hat and goes to work, churning out hopped whiskeys and smoked whiskeys and whiskeys made with all manner of obscure grains. All innovative distillers may be crazy to some extent, but there is a method to Bell's madness. His quinoa whiskey is not about to take America by storm. Whiskeys smoked over sassafras will never displace straight bourbon on the liquor store shelf. What they will do, though, is establish Corsair and distilleries that follow its lead as the anti-Beam, as companies that do the opposite of whatever the big outfits do – not as a counter-establishment pose, but as a matter of survival.

If a distiller spends years perfecting a whiskey as good as Buffalo Trace, Bell says, that would be quite an accomplishment. But the market isn't interested in another Buffalo Trace. It will, however, reward creativity, innovation, and uniqueness. And the pursuit of new styles and flavors is itself rewarding. Exploring new grains, new ways to age your bourbon, new ways to smoke or hop your whiskey – this is the sort of thing that should be driving new distillers.

The only reason to become a craft distiller these days is to produce something the market has never seen before. This book shows you just how to do that.

Clay Risen,
Author of "American Whiskey, Bourbon and Rye."

PREFACE

This book is an idea book. Let me explain. I became obsessed with photography for a while after college. It just kind of came out of nowhere. I wanted a book with lots of great ideas to try, and turn into small projects. I should have gone with a more serious tome going over the fundamentals of photography. I didn't. I went with a book called "The A-Z of Creative Photography." Every page had a new technique. You could just flip it open randomly, say to "Polaroid transfers" or "infrared photography" and just like that, you had a cool image of what the technique looked like and how to do it. I wanted a book that got me excited to shoot photos. That book became my adrenaline shot, my gasoline.

Everyday I would randomly flip it open to not just a new idea, but a new adventure, as I ran out into the world looking for something to photograph. I fell in love with that book. It was small enough to put in a camera bag, but big enough to show off the gorgeous images. It did not go too deeply into any one technique; that was not the point of it. It was like the game spin the bottle: you spin it and the randomness of life would throw you into some crazy situation. That is why I loved it. In my opinion craft distilling is in need of new ideas to create an authentic identity.

That has been the goal with this book - to make an "idea book" of different types of smoked whiskeys. A Kama Sutra of smoked whiskey positions for you to experiment with. There are much better technical books out there. You always need that technical competence, and there are some wonderful technical books out there. I highly recommend "Whisky: Technology, Production and Marketing" by Inge Russel.

The problem though, is that photography is well suited for this type of a book, because it is so visual. With whiskey, it is difficult to translate smell, taste, and mouthfeel into words. I have tried to make it as visual as possible, to make it inspire the creative side. When I was a homebrewer, I found such a book. Sam Calagione's "Extreme Brewing" was a fun book that made me more excited to brew beer than any technical book I had.

This book is focused primarily on smoking grains that go into whiskey. Its focus is not so much on distilling itself but on the ingredients and work before distillation that can make or break your whiskey. I got some flak for this in my first book, "Alt Whiskeys." It was criticized for being a 'recipe book' and collection of 'home brew recipes.' Those "home brew" recipes went on to win 92 medals at spirits competitions, including taking best of show at the ADI awards. Another one of those recipes won "artisan whisky of the year" in Whisky Advocate magazine.

Who is this book for?

This book is written for someone who is getting a new craft distillery off the ground, or for an established distillery wanting to create new products. One of my central themes in this book is that in general, the older the whiskey, the higher the rating. Except this trend does not hold in one critical area: smoked whiskeys. I believe there is a lot of new territory to explore in the world of smoked whiskeys. For a new or young distillery, you are just not going to have much aged whiskey for a very long time. Smoked whiskeys give you a chance to score higher in the ratings than you deserve, AND they are really awesome tasting. Why did peat become the dominant flavor in smoked whiskey production, when there are so many other smoke fuel sources? Also why have no American whiskeys experimented with smoke from hardwoods like hickory, mesquite, or apple? I hope this book inspires some distillers to forge new ground in the world of smoked whiskeys. There is a lot of room for experimentation.

The spirits

Myself, my cofounder Andrew Webber, distiller Andrea Clodfelter, distiller Clay Smith, and distiller Matt Strickland created about 80 different smoked whiskeys. Matt especially deserves thanks as he was the quarterback for many experiments. We also made a smoked rum, a smoked vodka, and a few smoked gins. We stuck to a simple all smoked malted barley base recipe. The barley was all smoked the same amount of time using different fuel sources. I used an emerson home pressure smoker, actually 4 of them, in sequence. I calibrated them often to make sure they were giving consistent results.

Corsair's smoked gin, named 'steampunk'

Nosings

I highly recommend you get third party professionals to taste your whiskey and give you honest feedback. I used two of the best in the business: Nancy Fraley and Julia Nourney. The nosings were written by Julia and Nancy, and that is intentional.

NANCY FRALEY
Distilled spirits blender and professional "nose" with a background in the American artisan/craft spirits industry. Nancy's focus is on custom blending, quality control, product assessment and the development of spirits.

JULIA NOURNEY
Julia is an international spirits consultant based out of Germany. She serves as a judge for international spirits competitions, writes about spirits, and consults for a number of spirits companies.

Why smoked whiskeys?

Our goal at the Corsair Distillery is to make unique and innovative spirits. Our motto is simple: If it has been done before we do not want to do it. We have a lofty vision: to expand the

> Our motto is simple: If it has been done before we do not want to do it.

horizons of whiskey making. How do we do this? By making distinctive whiskeys no one else has ever made. We have a number of alternative whiskeys, or as we call them: "alt whiskeys." An alt whiskey is any whiskey made outside the norm. We mostly focus on three types: unusual grains, smoked whiskeys made with something besides peated malt, and hopped whiskeys made from craft beer. With this goal in mind, we began looking at all the smoke flavors that had not been used in whiskey making. We have smoked rye whiskey, bourbon, malt whiskey, wheat whiskey, and whiskey made with unusual grains like amaranth, vodka, agave spirit, rum, and even gin. We make about 100 new recipes a year and pair them down to only a few that will become production whiskeys.

Why craft distillers should play with fire...

When we were first trying to get our distillery off the ground, we were obsessed with big smoky and peaty whiskies from Islay. We didn't have access to peat in Tennessee, but we had a lot of other great smoking materials, so we began experimenting. We wanted to create whiskeys that were distinctly Corsair and that would resonate as something unique with critics and fans alike.

Right from the start we saw a lot of our peers get beat up in the press for whiskeys that were supposedly too young or too harsh. Looking for some causality in all this we began to notice a curious trend in magazines, competitions, and whiskey judgings...

In general, we observed that the older the whiskey, the higher the score in the ratings. For a new distillery that is brutal. However, there is one area that this trend does not hold: heavily peated or smoked whiskeys. These whiskeys tend to score much higher than their age would belie, and they taste great. I personally prefer several of the newer heavily peated Islays to the far older, yet minimally peated whiskeys. After this revelation, we began really researching smoke and smoked whiskeys, as they score so much better than their age. We thought this was an area where craft distilling could contribute to the world of whiskey even with the hurdle of youth. It was shocking to see so few craft distilleries exploring this.

We noticed a lot of craft distillers really seemed focused on making a bourbon. That's great.

One of our first whiskey stills, a PDA-1.

We love bourbon. Unfortunately, that style of whiskey really shows off any flaws in fermentation and especially aging. I think it's probably the most difficult style for a new distillery to start with unless they truly have the time to let it age. We also noticed that consumers equate age with quality, which is tough for a new distiller. However, if you give someone a smoked whiskey, they tend to focus on the smoke character and judge the dram on the quality of the smoke, not the barrel. This is

> The older the whiskey, the higher the rating. However, there is one area where this trend does not hold: smoked whiskeys.

why from the very beginning we decided to focus on smoked whiskeys. This focus paid off in a big way when our Triple Smoke whiskey, made with cherry wood, beechwood, and peat smoked malts, won Whiskey Advocate magazine's "Artisan Whiskey of the Year" award. I encourage young, aspiring distillers to experiment with smoke whenever possible. I also encourage them to try to create new whiskeys that have never been made. Think outside the bourbon box.

American Whiskeys…where's the fire?

When I was first learning to distill, I decided to attend the Bruichladdich Distilling Academy, in Islay, Scotland. I got to try a lot of amazing Scotch with incredible smoke character. It made me wonder why there were no smoked American whiskeys. I was determined to make an American smoked whiskey when I got back to the States. Being from the South, where smoked meats are everywhere, making a smoked whiskey with all the woods and flavors readily available became a no-brainer.

If you look at the history of malting, all malt was smoked until the invention of indirect kilning in the 1800s. To dry out the malt to make beer and whiskey they burned whatever they had around, like peat, and whatever they burned left some smoke character on the final malt. The non-smoked malt was seen as being newer and superior. Changing tastes and the availability of different ingredients meant that a smoked American whiskey simply wasn't in the cultural cards. It still shocks me that no one in the South, while eating barbecue, thought to make a smoked whiskey with the abundance of hickory, oak, mesquite, cherry, and apple woods they had at their disposal. Now there are a few smoked whiskeys made by craft distillers, but they are still pretty scarce.

Smoking other spirit types

We have experimented with smoking other types of spirits besides whiskey. Two that I want to mention are gin and rum. I think these really work well because they are so unexpected for the spirit type. For the gin we actually smoked the botanicals and then put them in the carter head of our gin still. The carter head makes a lighter and more floral gin with less of the heavy oils. It also changes the smoke flavor, making a lighter smoke with less ashy creosote off flavors and more of the pleasant "distant campfire" aroma. For the rum we aged a molasses based rum in barrels that had contained a smoked whiskey. When we first distilled it, the rum was kind of boring and unremarkable. Interestingly, after some time in barrel, the smoke character really came through with very little whiskey character. The sweetness of the rum base really pairs nicely with the cherry wood and creates a wonderful complement.

Equipment

This book is focused on flavor, not smoking equipment. I noticed early in my home brewing days that the dudes who spent the most time messing with equipment brewed the least amount of beer. These gear heads often had mediocre beer and rarely won many awards at competitions. Some of the best homebrewers I knew often had "just ok" equipment. They were not always up on the latest, coolest, shiniest gadget, but instead spent all their time on brewing. I wanted to make the most beer and get really good at it. I have the same philosophy about smoking malt and making whiskey.

You can make ANYTHING into a smoker. The easiest smoker to make is this: put wood chips on a piece of aluminum foil, fold the foil to make a pouch, poke a few holes in the pouch and put that pouch on any heat source. You can also take a soldering iron (I buy them for $9 online and insert the hot tip into the foil pouch full of wood chips. However, there are a few things to be aware of. Most grills are meant to go above 225°F. Enzymes in malted barley necessary for breaking starches into sugar during brewing are heat sensitive and are denatured above 170°F. So in general you need to try and keep the grain under that temperature.

Most of the experiments in this book were done in Buchi Rotary Evaporator or Heart Magic oil still for distillation. The smokers I used were simple electric Emson home smokers.

One of our first gin still, a buchi rotovap

Smoke Flavor Types

We have made smoked whiskeys in five different categories: woods, barks, roots, herbs, and used barrels. We further break wood flavors into a couple of categories: hardwoods, fruit and citrus woods, and nut woods.

Fruit woods like apple, cherry, mulberry, pear, and nectarine have a distinct "sweetness" and are some of the most pleasant smoke smells. People who don't like smoked whiskeys will often still try these. They tend to be very aromatic and provide a lot of body to the whiskey. Their finish tends to be weak and therefore they work best, in my opinion, when paired with something else such as the more traditional hardwoods used for smoking: hickory, oak, alder, birch, ash, or mesquite. These are strong smoking woods that create a great base smoke character in the body and flavor of the whiskey, but usually are not as distinctive as some others. The nut woods like almond, macadamia, black walnut, and pecan add a nutty flavor and are distinctive but can sometimes become acidic in the finish.

Citrus woods like lemon and orange wood are some of the most unique flavors we have tested. They add an intense tropical fruit, oily, and citrusy smoke character to the whiskey. Even a little of this smoke can take over and dominate a whiskey, so these should be used in very small amounts for blending. At times they make the whiskey taste more like a gin. I recommend getting a third-party professional to give you honest feedback. I use two of the finest noses on the planet and highly recommend them: Nancy Fraley and Julia Nourney.

Hardwoods

alder	Hawaiian Guava	olivewood
almond	Hawaiian Kiawe	orange
apple	Hawaiian Ohia	peach
apricot	hickory	peat
ash	Jamaican pimento wood	pear
avocado	lemon	pecan
beechwood	lilac	persimmon
birch	macadamia	plum
black walnut	manzanita wood	red oak
crabapple	maplewood	sassafras
cherry	mesquite	white oak
cedar	mulberry	
grape	nectarine	

We have experimented with a number alt smoked whiskeys made with peat alternatives. Most of these have been made with wood. However, while researching the history of pipe smoking, I noticed an article claiming that Native Americans would cut their tobacco with herbs for flavor or for religious or ceremonial purposes. So we began experimenting with herbs, barks, and roots and smoking malt with them. The barks are similar in flavor to a lot of the woods. The roots are quite different and have an amazing range. Cascara and white willow are two of my favorites of all the fuels we have tried. The Jamaican dogwood bark tastes incredibly spicy, like the allspice the tree produces. The herbs can be incredibly distinctive and really bring out the character of the herb. For instance, sage is one of the most powerfully aromatic herbs in this entire group and the resultant whiskey is certainly true to the source.

Herbs/Roots

mullein	lavender	skullcap
angelica	lemon balm	spearmint
anise	licorice	sweet cicely
calamus root	mint	tarragon
catnip	mugwort	violet
clove	osha	wormwood
ginger	peppermint	
jasmine	sage	

Barks/Roots

bayberry root	catuaba bark	quassia bark
birch bark	fringe tree bark	white willow bark
blackberry root	Jamaican dogwood bark	dogwood bark
butternut bark	muira puama bark	yohimbe
cascara bark	prickly ash bark	willow

Another distiller asked if we had ever smoked malt by burning whiskey barrels themselves. We liked this idea and immediately experimented with different types of barrels. We actually call this the oak category as they are all made from the same wood species, Quercus Alba. Oak is a fantastic base smoke for building a smoked whiskey around. It is strong in the body but weak in the nose and finish. Oak is an amazing sponge and really absorbs the flavors of whatever has been stored in it. Wine barrels add great character to the nose of the malt and final whiskey. Tabasco®, is a brand of Louisiana pepper sauce that is actually barrel-aged for two years in oak barrels. Amazingly, the Tabasco character really comes through, making a striking spicy smoked whiskey with a peppery nose and a long spicy finish.

Barrel Woods

Cabernet barrel	French oak barrel
Bourbon barrel	Tabasco® barrel

Terroir

On the wonderful amazingribs.com blog, it is stated that trees, like grapes in winemaking, have a terroir. Essentially the place where a tree is grown is more important than the species. There is some truth to this. If you grew hickory trees in my native South and in Colorado, the soils and climate are so different that the resulting taste would probably be different. To quote the site: "Hardwoods have more minerals than softwoods, but, according to 'The Forest Encyclopedia,' their smoke flavor is influenced more by the climate and soil in which they are grown than the species of wood. This is very important to note, especially when you are caught up in the game of deciding which wood to use for flavor. This means that the differences between hickory grown in Arkansas and hickory grown in New York may be greater than the differences between hickory and pecan grown side by side."

However, in my research this is not the whole story. There are certain species so incredibly unique that the terroir is less a factor than the intense flavor. Coffee wood has such an intense coffee flavor that comes through. It is so distinctive that I cannot imagine the effect of terroir ever being as important. Lemon tree wood is the same. It is so intensely oily and citrusy that it often overwhelms most of the other flavors. There is certainly something to be said for the terroir, but the woods I have experimented with here have some major chutzpah.

MALT

History

"Malt is the soul of beer."

The invention of fire was possibly the greatest technological breakthrough in the history of mankind. The invention of techniques to create and control fire states it more accurately. Evidence of fire has been found in caves from over a million years ago. Fire allowed humans to stay warm, ward off night time predators, and cook food, which allowed many new foods to become digestible. It is no surprise that we have an incredible ability to taste smoke at very low levels.

For centuries, smoke flavor was common in the vast majority of malt, and therefore European beer and whiskey, which is distilled beer. For much of the history of beer and whiskey, smoke was a signature flavor. However, during the industrial age, the vast majority of these smoked malts disappeared. Why?

Although today some breweries and distilleries use unkilned, "green malt," the vast majority use kilned malt. Green malt has some great properties, like high enzymatic activity and being lower cost. However, green malts cannot be stored long without being dried in some kind of way. Kilning is tricky, as the faster you can kiln the better, but too hot and the enzymes will be destroyed. Kilning dries the malt, stops germination, makes it more brittle and easily milled, and makes it easy to separate the rootlets. Roasting the malt allows new flavors and color to be introduced. Kilned malts primary advantage over unkilned malt is it becomes a stable product that can be stored for a very long time.

Where malting began is unknown, though there is good reason to believe it began with the Egyptians. In villages in India and Africa, malting grains could be sun-dried, and "wind malts" were dried in European lofts. However, in many cold or damp climates, kilning with some heat source was necessary. They probably used whatever they could find and therefore an incredible diversity of smoked malts existed, and consequently, smoked beer.

Malting and brewing were both performed in individual households. Not only did every town and city have its own style of beer, but every home as well. In the 1500s malting and brewing began to separate as different professions and malt became more heavily supervised for purposes of taxation. By the 1700s smoke as a flavor had become perceived as a negative. Many different fuel sources were used, and straw was one that allowed a minimal smoke flavor. The cost of the fuel source, availability, flavor aspects, were all important to dictating which fuel source was used. Malt was dried directly over the fuel source by the heat, air, and smoke of the fuel source.

In the 1500s wood was becoming scarce in England and laws were enacted to make it more difficult to use. Coal was considered unusable, as the flavors associated with it would taint the malt. Coal was becoming more common in the rest of the process for brewing and distilling. In the 1600s a new fuel, anthracite, or Welch coal, which is purer than ordinary coal and has less sulphur, began to rise as a cheaper and more common fuel source for industry. It has almost no smoke. By the 1700s coke began being manufactured and used by brewers. Coke is made by taking low grade coal and heating it to remove impurities. In 1635, the first patent was granted for an indirectly heated malt kiln that would kiln malt without the smoke ever touching the malt surface. It worked by heating a furnace which then heated an air chamber above it, and this air was pumped up through the malt. This allowed all kinds of fuel sources to be used, whatever was the cheapest, thus forever changing the economics of malt... and the flavor.

Two of the reasons smoke began to change were technology and economics. Another was changing taste. The invention of pale malt at the end of the 1600s led brewing in a new direction. Smoked malts began to be seen as old fashioned, backwards, or poor in quality. The invention of the hydrometer in the early 1700s and widespread adoption allowed brewers to see just how much extract they were getting out of their malts. Pale malts delivered more final alcohol than darker malts, and thus there was an economic reason to further move to paler malts.

Another turning point for smoked beers was the invention of the patent malt. Patent malt is made in a drum roaster and roasted to a high degree. It becomes very dark and allows only a small amount of patent malt to be used to achieve the same brown color of a traditional porter. The brewer can use pale malts with just a small amount of patent malt for color, and thus dramatically increase the amount of beer made at a far lower cost.

In the world of whiskey, the invention of the coffey still allowed for inexpensive grain whiskeys. Different distilleries had different tastes. Blended whisky allowed for more uniformity of whiskey by mixing grain whiskey with single malts. This allowed a boom in whiskey, but further marginalized the smoke taste and flavor of whiskey.

However, in a few traditional holdouts, maltsters clung to tradition and kept making old fashioned smoked malts. In defiance of modernity or in keeping with tradition, maltsters in parts of Germany and Scotland stuck to the old ways of kilning their malt with smoke. In Germany, rauchmalt was made with beechwood and was responsible for a number of traditional smoked beer styles that have held on to this day, though tiny in volume. Unusually, these brewers often kept malting their own malts and brewing them under one roof, unlike the rest of the world. which had slowly separated out the malting and brewing as different crafts.

In Scotland, remote areas like Islay and the Hebridean islands have stuck with using peat for traditional peat smoked styles of whisky. Over the past few decades there has been a revival in heavily peated, smoked malts. Many whiskey enthusiasts, or peat freaks, have discovered the rich character and history of the iconic whiskeys of Islay, Skye, Jura, and the Scottish Islands. Heavily smoked whiskeys once looked on the verge of extinction but have now had a massive renewal of interest.

Smoke is cool again.

What is malt?

Malting is so important in making smoked beer and smoked whiskey that it deserves its own digression. There are so few whiskeys smoked outside of the malting process that it is unlikely the average consumer has ever tried one. With the exception of Balcones Distilling, Schlenkerla's distilled version of its rauchbier, or Corsair, I can't think of any commercial whiskeys that do not use smoked malt as the source of smoke.

Malting is the limited germination of cereal grains under controlled conditions for a specific purpose. That purpose for us is converting starches into sugars for brewing and distilling.

At its core, malting is an ancient process. Like brewing and distilling you can make it as simple or as complex as you want. Malting is the process of germinating a seed so that it releases enzymes critical to brewing, then kilning the seed to stop germination to lock in those important enzymes.

Malting involves a few distinct steps:

1) Steeping phase: when the grain is soaked in water.

2) Germination phase: when the seeds are allowed to sprout.

3) Kilning phase: when the grain is kilned to stop germination, and when the grain is smoked.

Floor malting at Laphroig

HOME MALTING

supplies

drilling the buckets

weigh grain dry

steeping

draining and cleaning

germination

couching

kilning

smoking

Initial malting
Most of the items needed for malting are simple and you probably already have in your home.

Malting your own grain

Initial Malting

If you've never malted your own grain, I suggest you do. It's easy and rewarding to see the process firsthand. It is a simple process that involves items you probably already have in your garage. This example will use barley, somewhere between five and ten pounds. Unmalted barley is commonly used as animal feed, so your local feed store or farmer's co-op is a good place to purchase unmalted grains. These are usually sold in 50lb bags. Homebrew shops and pet stores sometimes sell in smaller quantities. It's cheap, however, if you buy the "sprouting barley" commonly found in larger health food stores, you'll pay a premium.

What you will need:
Three 5 gallon buckets
distilled water
A drill
A 1/16" or smaller drill bit
A thermometer
Small scale
Optional: an aquarium pump with an airstone that is new, not used.
A cool dark place like a basement or a garage.
Barley that is not seed barley that is coated with a fungicide or pesticide.

Instructions:
Steeping
1) First weigh out the barley. You need to know how much you have.

2) Drill many small holes in the bottom of one of the buckets with the small drill bit to let water run through but not the grains, size the holes accordingly.

3) Using cold water of around 50 degrees, steep the grain. Make sure that the water is chlorine-free. This is because when you smoke grain, the chlorine and smoke can combine to form strange off flavors.

4) Change the water after 4 hours, then twice a day for two to three days. You can easily do this by setting the grain in the bucket with the drilled holes, and putting this bucket on top of another bucket. This way it holds water, and to change it just lift the top bucket out and all the water drains right out. You can add an aquarium pump to the water bucket which will help to keep the water oxygenated and by proxy, the grain as well. The aquarium pump and airstone allow you to change the water less frequently (once daily would suffice with this set-up).

Eventually, you will start to see small roots growing out of the grain kernels. These are called chits. The steeping phase ends when chitting can be seen on approximately 95% of the grains.

Germination

After the steeping phase, the grains will begin to germinate. The germination of the grains must happen in a cool dark space for two to five days. The best temperature for germination is in the mid-60s. Germination releases heat and too much causes several problems.

Drain the grain thoroughly and then put in a bucket in a cool dry place. The temperature needs to be monitored. Ideally the temperature of the germinating mass should be well under 70 degrees. If it is too hot it will encourage mold growth. The seeds will also germinate too rapidly, wasting enzymes. The grain must be turned several times a day to prevent heat build up, get rid of carbon dioxide, and prevent the rootlets from binding together. If using the aquarium pump, which will make the germination easier, you simply add the grain to the sieve bucket and place on top of a bucket with cool water that has had the airstone run into the water. This will keep the grain moist, aerated, and prevent heat buildup. The longer the germination period, the more highly modified the malt will be.

After about three days, the rootlets will have begun to grow and the acrospires, or shoots, will be visible. You continue malting until the small leaf, called acrospires, within the grain are approximately 75-100% of the length of the seed. You need to actually cut open the grain with a knife and look for the white leaf that is part of the endosperm and attached to the rootlets, as the acrospire is inside the grain. The external portion of the rootlet will be about 2x the length of the grain when it is ready, but measuring the actual acrospire length is the most accurate method to determine when to halt germination.

Once the rootlets are at the right length, it is time to "couch" it. Couching simply cuts off oxygen so the seed stops growing. You can simply put the top on the bucket and turn off the aquarium pump if you were using it. After a day it is time to kiln.

Kilning

The germinated, sprouted malt, or "green malt," is then moved to the kiln to dry. This is where smoke is added. This step stops all further modification of the kernel. If the malt is kilned at too high a temperature, the fragile enzymes will be destroyed. The amylase enzyme is destroyed over 170F. The main goal of kilning standard malts is to dry the malt as much as possible at lower temperatures (around 90°F), which helps preserve the enzymes in the malt. The easiest way to do this at home is to use an oven with the grain spread evenly onto trays. Many ovens don't operate at such a low temperature (90-120F) though sometimes an oven light is enough to reach the lower end of these temps.

The first drying period typically takes

Instead of manually turning you can use a concrete drum mixer on an electronic timer to turn your grain every four hours. These are cheap used as many people buy these and use them once.

about 24 hours, while the second drying period will typically last about 12 hours at a higher temperature of around 120°F. A third and final "curing" process will occur over the next 24-48 hours at approximately 180-220°F. The curing process influences the malt taste, aroma, and stability.

For smoked malt the smoking process begins during the kilning process. Start with green (wet, finished, but unkilned) malt. (Pale barley malt that has been soaked for 24 hours in cold water can be substituted for homemade malt.) Kiln it at the lowest setting until it is half dry. Sprinkle lightly with water and set aside for 12 hours. Soak mesquite, apple, or hickory wood chips overnight in water. You can experiment with different woods — each will impart a different character to your grains. Prepare a bed of coals in a traditional barbecue grill, or start a gas grill and set to low/medium. Drain the chips and place them in an even layer over the heat. Place the grains on a clean, fine-mesh screen over the fire. Cover the grill (leave the vents open) to get the full benefit of the smoke. Stir the grain every 5 minutes to prevent burning. Smoke the grain anywhere from 15 to 40 minutes until fully dry.

Finishing the Malt

Finally we have to do one more thing: remove the rootlets from the malt. The rootlets will add bitter off flavors that need to be avoided. Luckily, the rootlets will fall off rather easily with agitation. You can simply put the grains on top of a screen, shake the screen vigorously, and the roots will fall off. Some people pour the grain out of a bucket with a fan blowing and the lighter rootlets will get blown away. This can be a messy process so plan to do it outside or in a garage. Now you have standard malt. (Specialty malts such as crystal or roasted grains can also be produced at home, but require special techniques beyond the scope of this book.)

Andrea Clodfelter and Matt Strickland working in the interior of the Corsair Distillery, where the experiments in this book were performed.

Smoking Techniques

I have experimented with several whiskey smoking methods, all with their own strengths and weaknesses. Here are a few of the techniques:

Smoking the Malt

You can smoke your own malt and then brew your distiller's beer with it. When distilled, the smoke flavor comes over in the distillate, making a smoky tasting whiskey. This is a time tested process, but it's labor intensive and doesn't give the best yield of smoke flavor for the effort. However, this is the process whereby 99% of smoked whiskeys get their taste. If you are taking grain that has already been malted and smoking it, this is easy. The Bairds Malting Company in Scotland has said that rewetting pale malt and then smoking the malt can yield a very close approximation to standard smoked malt. If you are malting it from scratch and smoking it during the kilning phase, this is considerably more difficult. There is a saying, "there are many homebrewers of beer, but very few home maltsters." Malting is tricky, and not everyone has the patience for it. The feedback loop is slow, due to the time it takes, and thus it takes a long time to get good at it. This is the oldest form of smoke in whiskey and has centuries of use behind it. When making whiskey, it takes a lot of smoked malt to get the flavors to come through in the final whiskey. If you are using a rare fuel source, a hard to find or very expensive wood for example, this may not be the best route for producing smoked whiskeys.

Smoking malt is certainly the most common way of making a smoked whiskey, however there are other ways of doing it that deserve consideration.

Liquid Smoke

It is possible to add liquid smoke (not the BBQ product sold in the condiment aisle at your local grocery store), essentially smokey water, to the barreled whiskey. You make your own liquid smoke by forcing water and smoke to condense together (see Spray Condensation below). You get a lot of bang for your buck with this method. If you make your own smoke water and use it to cut down the whiskey from barrel proof to bottle proof then your smoke goes a very long way. You can use very little of your smoke fuel source for a lot of flavor, making this probably the cheapest method. The other advantage is that you get a lot of control over the final product. It allows you to achieve a higher level of consistency that would be difficult otherwise except for blending different batches. At the Schlenkerla brewery, different batches of smoked malt are mixed to achieve as much consistency as possible due to the fluctuations in the smoked malt. Since temperature and humidity can change the final smoke in the malt, it is easy to see how seasonally the malt will vary. Of course the wood is also a natural product and therefore has a lot of variation as well potentially causing further fluctuations in final smoke levels. However, it is a powerful technique and worth mentioning due to its economy and huge effect on the final whiskey.

Smoking the Barrels
This is an easy way to add smoke flavor. (Of course if you use barrels that previously held a smoked whiskey you can achieve the same effect. We recently put down some rum in a barrel that had contained one of our smoked whiskeys. It was amazing how much smoke flavor the rum soaked up and made for one of the best rums I have ever had.) If you took a new barrel and smoked it prior to filling it, the whiskey aged in the barrel takes on the smoke flavor immediately. This is very easy to do. You can take a simple gadget like food smoking gun and run the smoke into the bung hole. It is easy to drill two holes in a wooden bung, one for the incoming smoke, one for the exiting air.

Smoke Injection
This method uses a rheostatic pump to force smoke air through a stainless steel airstone into the liquid, either whiskey or water, at proofing/bottling.

Surface Transfer
This technique involves smoking barley or other grains, but then adding them to the whiskey in the barrel before bottling. It's a method that gives a fantastic yield for only a small amount of smoke, but certain woods can add sulfury off-flavors.

Surface Agitation
This is similar to putting smoke and whiskey in a martini shaker and shaking it to add the smoke. You can run smoke into the bottom of the condenser or use another vessel that allows you to add as much agitation to the whiskey as possible. If the whiskey is colder than the smoke you will get some decent smoke transfer.

Spray Condensation
This involves running the whiskey through a microdroplet spray over a smoke source, and then collecting the condensate. Great yield, but there is definitely a loss of "angel share" whiskey through evaporation.

Carter Head (Gin Head)
This is a distilling apparatus made for distilling botanical-based spirits like gin or absinthe. You put the juniper or other herbs in the gin basket and begin distilling your base spirit. The hot vapors will pass through the botanicals and pick up an extraordinary number of aromas and flavors. This device can also be used to produce smoked whiskeys by putting smoked malt into the gin basket and passing low-wine whiskey vapors through the malt.

Smoke variables

Most people opt to use some some type of smoked malt in the production of their smoked whiskey. If you plan on producing your own smoked malt, there are a number of factors that will influence the final smoke flavor and aroma of the grain that are important to consider. These include smoking temperature, humidity, fuel source, smoking time, and the type of smoking device.

Time

One of the most obvious variables is the length of time you smoke. I expected this test to be fairly linear, but I expected the longer it went there would be diminishing returns, meaning that as the surface of the cotton disc became darker, there would be less surface for new smoke to stick to.

Effect of length of time of smoke

0 minutes   5 minutes   30 minutes   45 minutes   90 minutes

However, I was wrong. As time went on the smoke seemed to pick up speed. The difference between 45 and 90 minutes is dramatic, even though 90 minutes is twice 45. The difference between 5 minutes and 45 minutes is nine times. But the color difference is not that dramatic to my eye. The difference between 30 minutes and 5 minutes, which is a multiple of six, was really minor. It seems like the smoke builds up a tacky layer of smoky goo that creates a tacky surface for more smoke to stick to.

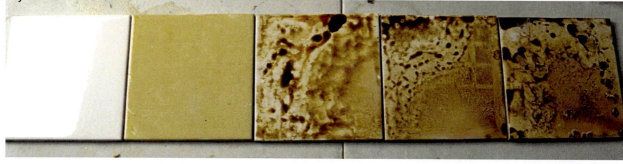

0 minutes   5 minutes   30 minutes   45 minutes   90 minutes

When I used white tiles, the difference was also interesting. From zero to five minutes the smoke creates a fairly even surface, but then after this develops, things just go crazy and the tiles look spattered with smoke. They really seem to grab an enormous amount of smoke after this initial layer is formed. Although there may not look like much of a difference in the photo between 45 and 90 minutes, when you touch the tiles, the layer on the 90 is quite thick, almost oily and certainly much thicker than the 45 minute tile. By smell the 90 minute is by far the smokiest.

Influence of the fuel source

You can see from the experiment above the dramatic effect that different fuel sources of smoke have on the material to be smoked. Here I used white cotton discs used for applying or removing make up. They were all smoked 45 minutes in the exact same model of smoker and placed in the same position. The smoker was the "Emson Electric Indoor Pressure Smoker 7 Qt ." I used several different types of fuel: a wood, a root bark like material, a dense herb, and then two different green herbs. They were all the same volume but differed a lot by weight. You can see the varying levels of dark smoke color the discs took on. The peppermint is by far the lightest color, and looks just slightly different than it did before I put it in the smoker. The smudges on the left are from my big clumsy and smoke grease covered hands. It is interesting how two herbs that are quite similar, the spearmint and peppermint, gave such different results.

Sensory evaluation

Darkness is not the whole story though. Although lighter in color, the peppermint disc smells more pronounced than the spearmint, even though the spearmint disc is darker. By far the smokiest disc to my nose is the pecan wood. Although the samples were the same volume, the pecan was the heaviest by weight. It's just the densest fuel here and that translated into a more intense smoke flavor. The angelica was the next heaviest by weight and had the second most smoke smell. That is not all though. I said the most SMOKE smell. The most intense smell overall was the cloves. The actual smoke smell of the clove sample was not that much but the clove smell was over the top. Looks can be deceiving.

Within the fuel source there are of course other variables. How long the wood has been seasoned, or aged, can play a huge factor in the smoke. The size of the wood particles changes the burn rate, temperature, and duration of smoke discharge.

SMOKED FOR 60 MINUTES WITH PECAN WOOD

DRY　　　　　　　　MOIST　　　　　　　　SOAKED

Humidity

The wetness and humidity of the surface of what is being smoked has a profound effect on the smoke adhesion, as the images above demonstrate. The dry disc is clearly the lightest in color. The moist disc is markedly darker, and looks more so in person than this photo shows. It also has a tacky feel when you pick it up. You can feel the smoke grease on the surface. The soaked disc is by far the darkest. The first disc was not wetted. The second disc was sprayed with a spray bottle. The third disc was submerged in water and shook out. Clearly moisture has an incredible ability to attract smoke.

Sensory evaluation

Without question the wettest disc had the strongest aroma overall. The medium moisture disc had the next highest amount of smoke smell. The dry disc was the weakest. Perhaps more importantly, however, was that there was a definite change in the type of smoke aroma. The soaked disc had an ashy, cigar smell to it while the dry disc had a cleaner campfire smell.

Temperature

The temperature of what you are smoking has a big effect on how well the smoke sticks as well. In the above pictures, two cans of soda were smoked. One was frozen solid prior to smoking and the other was allowed to sit at room temperature. Clearly the can with the ice cold soda in it absorbed a lot more smoke onto its surface. (The frozen can's top was opened so it would not explode during freezing.) Temperature can also have a big effect on humidity, which as we saw in the last experiment, has a pronounced effect on smoking grain.

Sensory evaluation

The smell of the frozen tile below is dramatically different than the room temperature tile. The smoke intensity is considerably higher, but the smoke flavor is also harsher and more ashy.

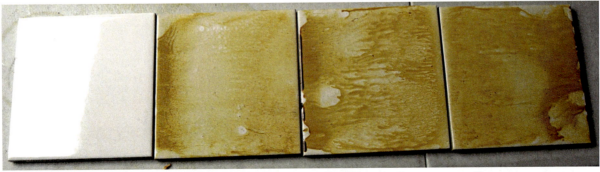

Original   Room Temperature   Refrigerated   Frozen.

Type of Smoker

The exact same model smokers had different smoking results, thus calibrating your equipment is very important for consistent results.

The type of smoker will obviously have an effect on the smoke as well. Gas fired, electric, pellet smoker, or wood fired all change the flavor, mainly because they burn their smoke fuels at different temperatures. Above you can see two smokers that are the same exact model number and they had been set to smoke for the same amount of time with the same weight of wood chips. I own four of these smokers. Early on I could tell one was just not smoking the same as the rest. It soon became apparent that it just was not burning as completely as the others. The example above is extreme, showing how one smoker was never completely burning the fuel source. I tried taking it apart and cleaning it. Eventually I just had to replace it. Now all four burn nearly identically. See the picture below of my test smokers.

The test smokers I used for many experiments in this book

Hickory wood in pellet, dust, chip,

	Hickory Pellets	Hickory Chips
Finished smoked malt		
Fuel Type		
Neutral Smoke Absorber		
Darkness levels in photoshop	64	54
Sensory Evaluation	Smokiest	Average Smokiness

and chunk form, all smoked for one hour

Hickory Sawdust

Hickory Chunks

50

39

Average Smokiness

Least Smoke Flavor

Fuel medium

Woods come prepackaged in a variety of forms. For example, you can buy hickory wood, a common smoking wood here in my native Tennessee, in many different formats. I can buy it in whole logs, split logs, chunks, chips, sawdust, as a super fine powder, and as industrial pellets. I believed the chunks would make the best smoke character with the most intensity. I was very dubious of the pellets. I was afraid the pellets, with them being so heavily processed, would change the flavor. They didn't, and informal taste tests around the distillery saw most people preferring the smoke they produced over the other available formats. A few were horrified to learn these were pellets. At the end of the day, the better taste wins. One nice thing is that now most pellets are made without binders. They use only pressure to form the pellets. This is because certain barbecue competitions will not allow anything that isn't 100% wood.

To soak or not to soak?

Most books on smoking meat say that you should soak your wood chips or chunks before smoking. In fact, one of the bags of wood chips sitting in front of me on my desk tells me to do just that. "Soak for at least 15 minutes" is the advice it gives. This is at best a waste of your time, but at worst can have bad consequences for your final whiskey.

The claim is that wet wood produces more smoke. The problem is that the water boils to steam. This can sometimes give the visual impression of a higher smoke density, when in fact it's the same amount of smoke with a lot more water vapor making It look like there is more smoke. Soaked wood can slow down the time of combustion, and this can be useful in some situations. It also releases more water vapor and therefore increases humidity which may also be useful. Depending on your smoker, the ambient humidity and temperature, and what type of fuel medium you're using, soaking the wood may or may not be benefical to you. (Regardless, I DO highly recommend you soak your grain before smoking it.) However if you decide to go this route, please make sure to use only chlorine-free water. If you soak your wood chips in chlorinated water you run the risk of creating off-flavors in your smoked malt that will come over during distillation.

Creosote Filtering

Creosote is composed of numerous compounds formed and held over from the burning of wood. When smoking malt it adds an ashy and sooty taste to the grain. I love a Lagavulin 16 single malt scotch, known for its ashy smoke character. Some people don't. You can change the character of your smoke by filtering it before it hits the grain. Sound hard? It's easy. I simply cover a smoking tray with a standard unbleached coffee filter. Smoke still goes through, but the larger burnt ash does not. I was afraid the coffee filter would ignite and while it never did, you should be cautious of this danger. I smoked two trays next to each other using pecan wood, one with a filter, one without. The difference was significant. The filtered was slightly less intense. However, the smoke character was much more pleasant and approachable. The filter-smoked grain has fewer harsh off flavors, however it must be smoked longer due to the loss of intensity.

Agitation

Grain is often smoked in flat trays with a mesh bottom that allows smoke to penetrate from below the grain bed. However, the deeper the grain bed, the more uneven the smoke in the final grain. As the depth of the grain bed increases it becomes harder for the smoke to penetrate and coat the grain in the middle of the bed. A way to smoke the grain more evenly is to use a drum smoker. It is a perforated stainless steel drum that the grain goes in and it spins slowly throughout the smoke session. For small scale testing I bought a small five pound coffee roaster drum on eBay. These are designed to be used with your home grill. They use a rotisserie chicken attachment to provide the constant turning motion.

Constantly turning the grain did result in more evenly smoked grain and better smoke intensity. However the drum set-up was expensive and a pain to use. It also took a while to get it to work correctly. We found that if it turned too slowly the grain wouldn't move enough to get good smoke expo-

A drum smoker that rotates the malt continuously results in more smoke flavor than a simple flat tray.

sure. If it turned too quickly the smoke blew away. In the end we did think it was worth pursuing as we now own a large scale version which you can see in the image below.

So when should you agitate?
If you are using a fuel that is hard to get, such as New Zealand manuka wood, then maybe the hassle is worth it. If you're doing very large batches where the difference of 20% more smoke can translate into a lot of money, then maybe it makes sense. Small batch smoking may not produce enough of a difference to make the hassle worthwhile.

For smoking large grain batches we now use this giant perforated lyco drum for Corsair's smoked whiskeys.

Smoke Loss
Smoke flavor and character are lost throughout the processes of brewing and distillation. It can be frustrating to put so much work into smoking barley and wind up with a beer or whiskey with very little smoke flavor. Smoke character can be lost during malt storage, mashing and lautering, fermentation, distilling, distillation cuts, and in the barrel.

At Corsair we first learned about smoke loss when we were struggling with a traditional rauchbier, a German beechwood smoked beer recipe we were trying to distill into a smoked whiskey. The final whiskey had so little smoke you had to strain yourself to find it. The smoked malt, or rauch malt, was not cheap and the final product left us less than thrilled. When we distilled it, some of the smoke was lost, and then the barrel seemed to take away even more smoke. Our friend Julia Nourney, who is one of the nosing experts I use throughout this book, was in the U.S. attending the American Distilling Institute conference in Louisville, Ky. She came by and smelled a bag of our Weyermann smoked malt. She was shocked by how little smoke aroma the malt had. She had just come from Germany where she had visited the exact malt house that had smoked our grain. She told us that the malt there had been intensely smoky, where as our malt was only faintly so. The fresh malt she was smelling in Germany had taken who knows how long to get to us, but somewhere along the way it lost a lot of flavor.

Storage

Smoked grain begins losing its aromatics as soon as it is packaged and placed into storage. During this time the main factors affecting smoke loss are exposure to air, time, humidity, and heat. The best ways to mitigate smoke loss due to storage time is to use the freshest malt possible and to store it using sealed bags with as little air space as possible. Most malting houses package their grain in bags that are slightly porous which can allow too much air to come into contact with the grain. This, in turn, potentially accelerates aroma loss. Briess uses foil-lined bags for their smoked malt to better lock in the flavor. If any maltsters are reading this, I highly recommend you do the same. If we know the malt won't be used for a few weeks, we will place it in cold storage at 45°F and low humidity.

Mashing/Lautering

When malt is brewed and transformed into wort, there is a loss of smoke character. We lauter and ferment off the grain, essentially filtering out the grain husks and fermenting only the liquid wort. When we take the spent grain husks and dump them, there is an intense smoke aroma that seemingly didn't make it into the wort. However, sparging with hotter water seems to pull more smoke flavor into the wort.

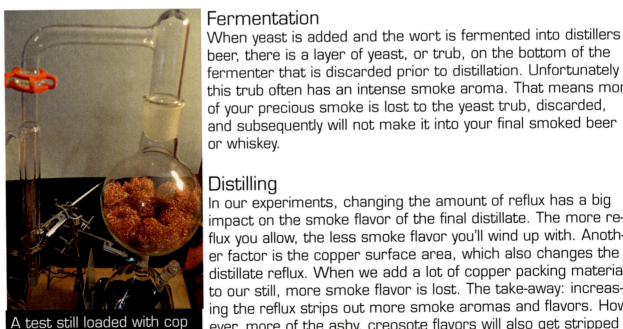

A test still loaded with copper mesh in the carter head area of the still

Fermentation

When yeast is added and the wort is fermented into distillers beer, there is a layer of yeast, or trub, on the bottom of the fermenter that is discarded prior to distillation. Unfortunately this trub often has an intense smoke aroma. That means more of your precious smoke is lost to the yeast trub, discarded, and subsequently will not make it into your final smoked beer or whiskey.

Distilling

In our experiments, changing the amount of reflux has a big impact on the smoke flavor of the final distillate. The more reflux you allow, the less smoke flavor you'll wind up with. Another factor is the copper surface area, which also changes the distillate reflux. When we add a lot of copper packing materials to our still, more smoke flavor is lost. The take-away: increasing the reflux strips out more smoke aromas and flavors. However, more of the ashy, creosote flavors will also get stripped out, so promoting some reflux during distillation may be a good idea if you are looking for a cleaner distillate.

Distilling Cuts

Another problem during distillation is that a lot of smoke flavor is lost to the heads and tails cuts, which are discarded. The tails are the primary culprit here with a lot of smoke aroma coming over near the end of the run. There isn't an easy way to correct this without getting into overly complicated cutting techniques. We typically alleviate some the smoke loss though by re-distilling the heads and tails and adding the resultant distillate back into the rest of the high-wines. This "recovery run" typically reclaims a fair amount of smoke character.

Distillation can give you a chance to add back some smoke character, however. We have a carter head still, used for gin making. It has a simple stainless steel gin basket attached to the column where you can add gin botanicals. If you add smoked grain to the gin basket and turn on the still, distillate will run through the grain bed and extract the smoke flavor on the grain surface. Our gin still allows us to divert the distillation stream through the gin basket when we want to. We wait until the heads cut is done to maximize smoke flavor in the hearts of the still run. This is an easy way to add back smoke and it targets just the hearts of your run. It also gives a lighter and more pleasant smoke character with very little ashy or petroleum flavors. However, proper cuts should still be made and monitored, as letting the run go too long can still produce a lot of off flavors in the finished spirit.

Barrel Loss

You should expect some smoke loss in the barrel. Anytime you smell smoke somewhere not in your final whiskey or beer, you have lost smoke flavor. If you smell a freshly emptied barrel, you will be amazed at how smoky it is and what a sponge for flavor the barrel wood can be. We made a smoked rum by simply filling one of our spent Triple Smoke 15 gallon whiskey barrels with freshly distilled rum. Within a week the smoke level of the rum was impressive, and within a month it was intensely smoky.

Bottling

During bottling the whiskey is proofed down from barrel proof, usually about 120 or more proof to 80 proof. When cut down with water, the smoke flavor is diluted. This needs to be factored into your final whiskey. You can make a smoke water and cut your whiskey with this instead of just pure water to keep the flavor. If this will be a commercial product the federal TTB, the Alcohol and Tobacco Tax and Trade Bureau which manages spirits labels, may require it to be called a "flavored" whiskey. There are many ways to make smoked water. One of the easiest is to put ice in your smoker and run it normally with a collection tray below to grab the melted ice, which will become smoky flavored water.

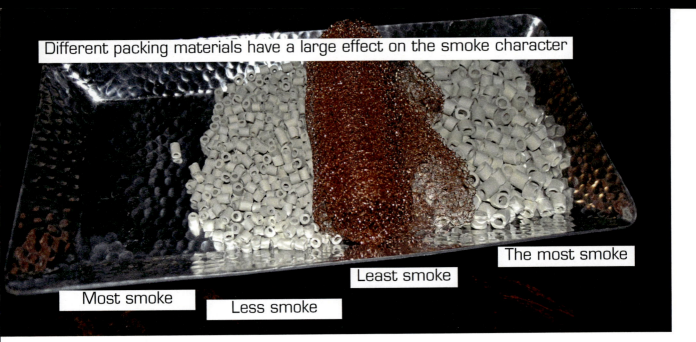

Different packing materials have a large effect on the smoke character

1. Daniels, R. and G. Larson (2000). Smoked beers : history, brewing techniques, recipes. Boulder, Colo., Brewers Publications.
2. The free dictionary. http://www.thefreedictionary.com/peat
3. Dr. P. Bossard. Jan. 9, 2007. Peat, Phenol, and PPM. http://www.whisky-news.com/En/reports/Peat_phenol_ppm.pdf
4. Ruiz, Alvin C. (2011-06-01). Scotch: The History and Enjoyment of The Most Popular Spirit (Kindle Locations 169-170). . Kindle Edition.
5. Russell, Inge,Stewart, Graham. Whisky: Technology, Production and Marketing (Handbook of Alcoholic Beverages). Academic Press; 1 edition (July 10, 2003)
6. Macdonald, Fiona (2012-01-04). Whisky, A Very Peculiar History (Kindle Locations 452-456). Salariya. Kindle Edition.
7. Teemu Strengell, 2/13/2011. Whisky Science Blog. http://whiskyscience.blogspot.com/2011/02/peat.html
8. Teemu Strengell, 5/29/2011. Whisky Science Blog. http://whiskyscience.blogspot.com/2011/05/peat-terroir.html

GRAIN TYPE EFFECT ON SMOKE CHARACTER

Corsair's Clay Smith turning locally grown Carolina barley at the Riverbend Malting company

Different types of grain smoke differently.

Different grains seem to absorb smoke character to varying degrees. Currently the vast majority of whiskey (and beer) is made with four grains: barley, wheat, rye, and corn. Of the core four grains, barley is the best for smoking, with wheat second, rye a distant third, and corn being almost impossible to smoke.

However, there are other interesting grains, some old, even ancient, that distillers should consider if they want to expand whiskey's horizons. This may be for reasons of taste, practicality, cost, or even for sustainable reasons. When creating a new whiskey recipe, or modifying an old one, these grains give more options to the distiller in terms of the final spirit. Some grains have been used in alcoholic beverage production in other cultures, like buckwheat, millet, and Job's tears, but not commercially in western culture. Let's look at a couple of potential alt grains in detail.

Oats

Oats were the predominant brewing cereal in the middle ages, but have now lost their significance. Oats have a long history in brewing beer, yet are virtually nonexistent in the history of distilling for whiskey. Whiskey is distilled beer. To a distiller, beer is simply whiskey that has not reached its true potential. The better the beer, the better the whiskey right? Oats have high protein, lipids, fats, and gums that change the mouthfeel of the whiskey and add a pleasant oatmeal like sweetness, though it is much more subtle than the mash. Oats are also extremely economical and readily available. When distilling, we never know what is going to come over, and what is not. We were surprised when some of the creamy body came across in the distillate just like an oatmeal stout beer.

Quinoa

Quinoa is a grain from the Andean region of South America. It was first cultivated there about 7000 years ago. Historically it was used to make chicha, an undistilled, fermented beverage with a low alcohol content. Quinoa is actually is more closely related to beets and spinach than other cereal grains. It adds an earthy and nutty flavor to whiskey. Quinoa can be bought as either red, black, or white seeds. The red and black have more character, but are harder to source. It can found in malted form more easily than other alt grains, as it germinates easily and quickly. Like corn, it requires a cereal mash, or boil step, making for a longer mash day. It can grow in very poor soils and with no fertilizer, so it has a reputation as being more sustainable and green than traditional grains. Of the alternative grain whiskeys we have made at Corsair, this one generates the best feedback in terms of taste.

Spelt

Spelt is an ancient relative of modern wheat that has been grown since the Bronze Age. It has a nutty flavor that has seen its revival amongst health food advocates and has dramatically increased in popularity in the past two decades. When malted, it is similar to wheat in terms of ability to convert starches to sugar. It has less gluten than wheat and less viscosity. This makes it better for brewing, yet weaker for baking. Its taste in whiskey is similar to wheat with more of an earthy, toasted bread smell.

Triticale

Triticale is a new grain variety created by crossing certain species of wheat and rye to create a grain with the hardiness of rye and the yields of wheat. Malted triticale is similar to malted rye and has been identified as a grain with great promise for the brewing and distilling industry. Malted triticale has high diastatic power and a very low gelatinization temperature. Triticale can mash without prior boiling. In terms of taste, it does have the spicy character of rye, but less pronounced. This is a fascinating grain with a lot of potential.

Milo
Sorghum, often called milo, is a type of grass that produces both a sap that can be made into a sweet syrup, and a grain. It is the only plant I know of with the potential to make both a rum, from the sap, and a whiskey, from the grain. It has been studied as a potentially important crop for fuel ethanol. This grain tends to be cheap, easy to source, and fairly easy to work with. When malted it has a much lower diastatic power than barley, so it needs to get its enzymes from somewhere else.

Buckwheat
Buckwheat has been used in several craft beers and some Japanese shochu, but not in whiskey making. This is a shame because it adds a great nutty flavor that is quite distinctive. The taste is somewhat similar to pistachios when roasted.

Buckwheat can be malted easily, but has significantly lower enzymes for starch conversion than barley, usually less than a third. Buckwheat is gluten free, and thus important for people who are gluten intolerant.

Millet
Millet is a small seeded cereal species grown all over the world for food. It grows well in difficult environments and is extremely resistant to drought, making this an excellent survival food if a main crop fails. In my native Tennessee, there is an oral history of moonshiners using millet when the corn crop was lost. Millet was usually planted by hunters to attract waterfowl, but it also was appreciated for its hardiness and flavor. Many of these old timers believed this was a superior moonshine, smoother than corn. It can be difficult to work with, which may explain why it has never

been commercially used in distilled spirits production in North America. Millets are traditionally important grains used in brewing millet beer in some cultures, for instance, in many African countries. Millet is one of the easiest grains to source and is quite inexpensive, but also frustrating to mill, due to its small size. Traditionally it could only be found unmalted, but recently the Colorado Malting Company has started making and selling malted millet for breweries in the Colorado market.

Blue Corn
Blue corn is prized for making corn chips due to its superior taste. Bourbon made with blue corn

instead of the standard flint corn has a richer, nuttier flavor profile. The spirit just has more character. Blue corn can be more difficult to brew, as it is higher in oil and protein. It is

always strange mashing it as the mash turns bright purple, sort of an eggplant color. A bourbon is by definition 51% or more corn. When experimenting with this whiskey style, this is typically a huge limitation in creating new recipes. Blue corn bourbon that uses this grain makes for a different taste profile while still being true to bourbon.

One grain I have not been able to get my hands on, but has a lot of potential for distillers, is tritordeum. This very new grain is a cross between wheat and barley and has one extremely exciting characteristic. It has a higher diastatic power, meaning the enzymes to convert starch, than barley. In fact it has the highest diastatic power of any cereal grain currently being considered for beer production. Why is this important? Well, let's say you wanted to make bourbon with as much corn as possible to push the corn taste (or save money), but did not want to use artificial enzymes. You could use a lot less tritordeum than barley to convert the corn starches, allowing you to push the amount of corn in the whiskey's mash bill.

It can be difficult to source many of these grains, which may explain why distillers have not embraced them. Sourcing them in malted format is even harder. Several micro malting companies have recently introduced malted versions of these grains. Rebel Malting in Nevada now offers malted millet, emmer wheat, and buckwheat. Valley Malt has a smoked triticale, and the Colorado Malting Company makes malted millet, teff, quinoa, and buckwheat.

Grainarchy

Alt grains work best in concert, rather than alone, in my experience. Corsair recently had the honor of winning the top award at the American Distilling Institute's competition with "Grainiac," a nine grain bourbon. This bourbon pulled together many previous experiments with grains resulting in a very complicated bourbon using corn, rye, wheat, barley, buckwheat, triticale, spelt, oats, and quinoa. The judges really enjoyed it and this is where I think alt grains work best, in complementing each other. Just as master blenders add small amounts of different whiskeys to add different notes of flavor, by using all these grains in small amounts the sum was greater than the parts. It was more balanced. Grainiac benefited from the mouthfeel of the buckwheat and oats, and the nutty and earthy character of the quinoa, spelt, and triticale.

Alternative types of barley, wheat, and rye

Beyond exotic grains like quinoa and buckwheat, there are versions of the standard malts most distillers never use. If you look at the types of malted barley most brewers use when making a new beer, they have over 70 different types of malt at their disposal. Most distillers however, just use plain two row barley. This is a shame as there are some great malts which can really add a lot to a whiskey. Chocolate malt adds a rich coffee like cocoa flavor. Caramel 120 adds some great roasted caramel flavor with hints of burnt sugar and raisins. Caramel 60 adds toffee flavors which pair nicely with the char of the barrel. Unmalted, roasted barley adds toasted, biscuit, and sourdough flavors to the whiskey. Honey malt adds a sweet honey like smell. Chocolate wheat and chocolate rye also add strong toffee like and chocolate flavors. Distillers have typically not used these as they have a lower yield, but it does not take much of some of these malts to add extra flavor.

So how do these grains compare when it comes to smoked whiskeys?

You can see in the following page table that only malted quinoa tops barley for smoke. Rolled oats also work quite well, but just not quite as well as barley.

Intensity was based on a simple and informal 10 point scale.

SMOKE ABSORPTION OF DIFFERENT GRAIN TYPES

Grain	Intensity	Notes
Malted barley	9.5	Triticale performed poorly.
Wheat malt	5	Wheat just does not seem to soak up smoke the way barley does.
Corn	1	I have terrible luck with smoking corn. I can never get it to smoke, not sure what MB Rolands's secret is.
Rye malt	2	Rye malt's odd surface just does not seem to soak up the smoke flavor.
Millet	1	I expected more from millet, but its tough outer shell seems to be a poor surface for smoke adhesion.
Quinoa	2	Quinoa was a shocker. Whole quinoa performed terrible.
Malted quinoa	10	Malted quinoa however, barley seemed to edge out barley in terms of most smoke. The explanation may be that the saponin surface is washed off during malting.
Oats, whole	2	Oats performed terribly in the whole form.
Oats, rolled	8	Rolled oats worked much better than whole oats in terms of soaking up smoke flavor.
Buckwheat	2	Buckwheat, whole, did not perform well. This is a shame, as this grain adds some great flavor to the mash.
Amaranth	2	Amaranth's tiny seed size makes it difficult for smoke to penetrate and soak up much flavor.
Triticale	3	Triticale performed poorly.
Spelt	4	Spelt performed slightly worse than it's cousin wheat.
Sorghum	5	Sorghum performed mediocre overall.

EXISTING SMOKED MALTS

Currently there are only four smoked malts that you can readily buy in North America: a cherry wood smoked malt from Briess; a peat smoked malt from Scotland by Simpsons, and a beechwood smoked malt from Weyermann in Germany. Weyermann recently released a new oak smoked wheat malt for enthusiasts of ancient beers like the Gratzer. If you are looking to make smoked beer or whiskey, I suggest you study these malts before smoking your own grain. Here is a little more info on these malts:

CHERRY WOOD SMOKED MALT (BRIESS ®)

Produced in America's heartland, this Briess specialty grain is smoked with a proprietary process using cherry wood to deliver a unique, enzyme-active malt. Boasting high enzyme activity and diastatic power, this Kosher-Certified malt delivers a smooth, sweet, smokey flavor at a modest 5 Lovibond, without any astringent phenolic harshness. Smoked in small batches to give a consistent smoked flavor. We at Corsair have had a lot of success with this malt. It adds great character.

PEAT SMOKED MALT (SIMPSONS ®)

Produced in the UK, this malt has been lightly peated to enhance the flavor, where peat moss is gently smoked over slow-burning coals outside the kiln during kilning, allowing vapors to drift above the malt. Typically scoring around 2.5 Lovibond, this malt should deliver a very light yellow color and a very intense flavor of iodine and seaweed smoke with a phenol level ranging between 12 and 24.

BEECHWOOD SMOKED MALT (WEYERMANN ®)

Often referred to as "rauchmalt," this beechwood-smoked German specialty grain is well-known for its use in the famed "Bamberger Rauchbier" style of beer. Offering excellent extracts at low moisture, this malt scores around 2.8 Lovibond, contributing a light color to beer, along with the classic German smoked flavor and aroma.

OAK SMOKED WHEAT MALT (WEYERMANN ®)

This malt has arrived just in time as craft brewers and home brewers are rediscovering classic German beer styles like Grätzer, Lichtenhainer and beers from northeastern Europe that were traditionally 100% wheat malt. The Oak smoked wheat malt can add a wonderful smoky taste to just about any beer you make. Oak smoked wheat malt is made from German grown top-quality spring wheat.

NEW SMOKED MALTS ON THE HORIZON?

There is a lot of creativity coming out of the new craft malting movement. Three recently launched companies have plans to make new and unusual smoked malts. On the next few pages you can learn more about Valley Malt, Riverbend Malting, and the Colorado Malting Company. Valley Malt recently made a maple smoked triticale malt. Colorado Malting has been making a cottonwood smoked malt. Riverbend is currently working on a floor-malted smoked malt using locally sourced grains but has not released any details as of this writing.

Beer & Ingredients II, The Ultimate Beer Ingredient Guide, What does What. Take your home brew to the next level, homebrew's ingredient guide. (Kindle Locations 1205-1218). (2012-01-16). Freedom of Speech Publishing, Inc.. Kindle Edition.

CRAFT MALTSTERS

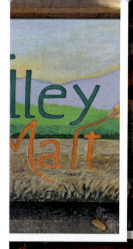

Valley Malt's debearder

The Stanleys

The author touring Valley Malt with maltster Andrea Stanley

VALLEY MALT

Innovative craft maltster Valley Malt has been making malt for three years in Hadley, MA. Husband and wife maltster duo Christian and Andrea Stanley have experimented with a variety of smoked malts. They are currently making a maple smoked triticale for Corsair, which sadly was not finished in time for this book. However, this is a great company to reach out to for unusual smoked malts.

Manually turning the grain

Valley Malt's seed cleaner

Malting vessels

CRAFT MALTSTERS

RIVERBEND

Riverbend's passion is in using local grains in the most basic of malting techniques: floor malting. They are planning on releasing some smoked malts in 2014 using locally sourced hardwoods to make smoked malts for brewers and distillers.

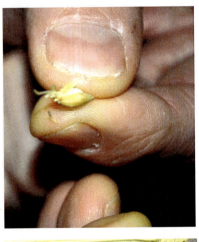

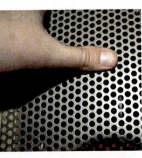

CRAFT MALTSTERS

COLORADO MALTING

"Field to glass" is the motto for the Colorado Malting Company, and it fits for this farm-based maltster. They use a variety of unusual grains like teff, buckwheat, and quinoa. They have a cottonwood smoked malt they smoke in modified 55 gallon drums. The cottonwood has a pleasant and sweet nose similar to pear wood smoked malt than a hardwood like hickory.

Peat is the most common fuel for smoked whiskeys, but due to its source and form, it doesn't quite fit in with the other fuels mentioned so far. It is so important that it deserves a quick digression.

What is peat?

Peat is pure awesomeness when it comes to Scotch whisky. It adds a great smokey flavor that makes certain whisky really stand out. Peat gives whisky character and adds so many of the things I love about smoked whiskey: the smells of campfire, the outdoors, and a rich meaty taste. But what is it? Here is a quick boring definition:

peat1
n 1.a. a compact brownish deposit of partially decomposed vegetable matter saturated with water: found in uplands and bogs in temperate and cold regions and used as a fuel (when dried).

Peat is essentially decayed plant matter that looks, well, like mud. When dried it can be burned and used as a fuel source. The resulting smoke, called reek, is critical to the kilning of some whisky barley malts and imparts a strong character to the final grain. Peat forms in bogs or moors and in acidic and waterlogged areas that favor the growth of moss. When the plants die they decompose at an incredibly slow rate due to the lack of oxygen, and accumulate in layers. Because it decomposes so slowly, the carbon is not released as carbon dioxide. The peat is dark black because of this high level of carbon, which is why it such a great source of smoke and heat.

> **Reek:** reek is the smoke from burning peat.
> **Reek Geek:** someone obsessed with peat smoke, like the author. Actually I just made up this term.

Peat is common in many northern countries. It is typically cut with spades and dried. Peat is central to the identity of certain styles of whisky, and is most closely associated with the Scottish island of Islay. Islay is home to some of the most famous distilleries on the planet: Ardbeg, Bowmore, Bruichladdich, Bunnahabhain, Caol Ila, Kilchoman, Lagavulin, Laphroaig, and Port Charlotte. There are other distilleries that also have a strong peat smoke taste, like Talisker, but Islay is the region most closely associated with peat.

Why is it so important to Scotch whisky?

Peat was used as a fuel source to dry barley and fire stills for distillation until the 1960s.

Peat Regions
Peat for whisky making comes from a few distinct regions in Scotland: Islay, Orkney, and the North East region. The different areas influence the taste of the peat. Factors such as location, climate, and humidity change the character of the peat, and therefore the final whisky. Islay peat is typically richer in smoky phenols. The cutting depth also influences the character as different phenol levels, nitrogen, and carbohydrate content vary depending on the depth of the cut.

Malting with peat
At one time all malted barley had a smoky flavor, as it was not until the invention of indirect fired malting that malts could be made with no smoke character. Some fuel sources were available that had almost no smoke character, such as hay. However hay was an impractical fuel for large quantities of malt. In the old days, the malt was dried directly over the fuel source, or fire. Later malt house kilns fed the warm smoke air up through the kiln to dry the malt. In indirect firing, cheaper fuel sources like coal, coke, or petroleum were fired and exhausted outside of the kiln. The heat was captured and indirectly dried the malt with no smoke ever touching the malt.

Examples of ultra high ppm whisky
The amount of peat in a whisky is expressed in PPM, or parts per million. Lately, due to the enthusiasm of peat freaks, whiskey lovers who have a passion for peated malts, there has been a battle amongst several distilleries to see who could make the most intensely peated whisky. Below are some examples of some of the most heavily peated whiskeys in the world.

An American Peat Whiskey?
On the following page I showcase an interesting American whiskey using Canadian peat smoke.

Their hand built smoker in action!

An American Peated Whiskey?
The inventive duo of Bryan Davis and Joanne Haruta launched Lost Spirits Distillery and have been making peat smoked whiskeys...in America. They use Canadian peat in their handmade smoker. They also built their still themselves and it is one of the coolest I have ever seen. At 110 ppm, their whiskey Leviathan is one of the most heavily peated whiskeys in the world and really shows the exciting experimentation coming out of craft distilling.

Canadian peat is used to smoke the malt.

INTRODUCTION TO NON-PEAT SMOKE PROFILES

On the following pages are the many different smoked whiskey experiments we have created. The experiments were exactly the same except for the smoke fuel source used to smoke the barley. The following pages are arranged by fuel source type: wood, herbs, barks, roots, and used barrels.

Who wrote the nosings?
The whiskey nosings were made by Julia Nourney and Nancy Fraley, two of the best noses in the industry. I did not write them. It is important to rely on others who are more objective. I am using their notes, unadulterated, except for punctuation errors. This is because nosing is a very subjective experience. The order of words is very important as they are the strongest, initial impressions. If you are not used to reading whiskey notes it may seem like some form of stream of conscious beat poetry written while tripping on hallucinogens. Because it kind of is. It's important to get the overall impression. I gave them "control" samples of unsmoked whiskey as a comparison and asked them to focus on the smoked flavor and spend less time on the barrel, fermentation, and grain character.

I have spent a lot of time sourcing woods, smoking barley ,and writing about it so that you can learn what I have. However, in a perfect world you, the reader, could smell and taste these creations for yourself. The sensory experience is the weakest thing about this book, and until someone invents smell-o-vision, it is just what it is.

How these whiskeys were made
Grains
Two row pale barley malt, which had already been malted, made by the Rahr corporation was used. The barley was always soaked the same amount of time (four minutes) in identical stainless steel sieve trays.

Fuels
The different fuel sources were never presoaked. I used them dry. I tried to buy wood seasoned for a year or more, but sometimes with the more exotic woods I had little information about the source. This is always a problem with sourcing woods. WARNING: never use wood scraps or wood from an unknown source, as many woods are treated with harmful preservatives.

Equipment
The small batches of these experiments were all done in Emson electric five quart smokers. A 4.75" diameter stainless steel, fine mesh flour sifter sieve was used to put the fuel source in, by volume. This is a problem, as most smokers are equipped to handle materials by volume, and different fuel sources have different amounts of density. Loose materials do not perfectly fit in these trays.

Definition of terms
In the following pages you will see many references to "NPFC." Nose, Palate, Finish, and Conclusion are what whiskeys are judged by internationally in competitions and in trade publications. These 4 are very important to perceived quality of the spirit and every distiller should pay attention to all steps of how the consumer judges whiskey.
Nose: the "N" stands for the nose, which is how the spirit smells and is the moment in time before the spirit is actually put into the mouth. It is customary for people to smell

the whiskey in the bottle, glass, or the stopper, before they taste it. This builds anticipation. This step starts the moment the bottle is opened as some whiskeys are so powerful that the whole room will smell like whiskey.

Palate: this is when you drink the whiskey. How it feels in your mouth, the mouthfeel. This lasts until you swallow the whiskey. This is wat the casual whiskey drinker thinks is important. But to judges, they are looking at more.

Finish: This describes the sensation after you have swallowed and the long burn that follows after the drink is down. This can burn for a few seconds or last a bit longer if an oily smoke fuel source is used, like lemon wood. After the whiskey is swallowed you are still smelling and tasting the spirit.

Conclusion: This is the overall impression you are left with after the finish fades away.

Differences between judges
American and European judges tend to have differences in judging. Julia is German, Nancy is an American. Julia wrote about her thoughts between the differences in American and European judges, which I want to include:

From Julia Nourney:
After finishing the sampling I had a look at the tasting notes of my colleague and friend Nancy, just to find out if we both have similar feelings about these whiskeys. And while I was comparing our notes I realized that we mostly have the same basic thoughts about sweet, sour, bitter, etc. but we both made totally different experiences while we grew up and developed our sensory. It was not just that our mothers fed us different things; it is the whole eating culture that divides both sides of the pond.

It made me smile to read how many different barbecue and tomato sauces or sandwich spreads Nancy knows and how she described it. We don't have such products in our shops and the few American brands we can buy here are mostly available in specialist shops. Nancy also mentioned so many different dishes which I have never heard of but I am quite sure that you, dear reader, are familiar with. And on the other hand I am quite sure that there are many dishes and flavours I have mentioned that you are not aware of. And additionally it might also be a language problem because I am not a mother tongue speaker (which – I am sure – you have already found out) what probably makes it extra difficult for you to follow my impressions.

I sometimes work as a judge for spirits competitions and it is always interesting to have Americans in the panel because they judge spirits completely different than judges from Europe or Asia do. Americans are very well known (and also feared) for judging obvious aromas quite high while judges from other parts of the world prefer mostly subtle and sometimes even hiding aromas. That might make it easier to understand why some products are different successful here and there.

This is also the reason why I think that the evaluated whiskeys here satisfy the American taste better than the European one because some of the flavours are so striking that they tax European tongues. On the other hand I am sure that most aromas in these whiskeys open up a new dimension to people who have never had such an experience. … and this is probably one of the most enjoyable things in life! Don't miss it!

ALDER WOOD
Alnus tenuifolia

Alder chips

Alder logs

Description
The alder tree is deciduous (sheds its leaves annually) and common in North America. The wood is often used for smoking fish, but is incredibly versatile, and is often used for pork, beef, poultry, and even cheese. The biggest commercial user of alder wood is the fishery industry, and this is how most people are familiar with it. It grows near water and is especially abundant in the Pacific Northwest. It has a reddish tint reminiscent of cedar wood.

It has a light, sweet flavor but less sweet than fruit wood species. The sweetness keeps the smoke from becoming too bitter, resulting in a very clean flavor. It is less dense than other woods and therefore tends produce fewer acrid and ashy off-flavors. Anyone enthusiastic about smoke should get to know this wood because it is so versatile. It makes an excellent "base" smoke that can get accents from other places or it can be used all by itself. This wood should be in everyone's toolkit.

Tasting Notes - NF
Nose: Smoke, smoke everywhere… the whiskey's going up in flames. Oh, the humanity! The first impression is an intensely smoky mezcal with a touch of ethyl acetate fruitiness, spicy cinnamon, very mesquite-like, bright.
Palate: Again, very reminiscent of a sweet, smoky mezcal, but oh so delicious! Still somewhat bright and fruity, with the smoke being similar to mesquite.
Finish: Wow, what an incredibly long finish. The sweetness of the smoke dries out, but the smoke goes on for a long time.
Conclusion: This seems more like a distillate produced from wild variety of agave (such Tobala, Tepeztate, or Espadin) than a malt, so it would be very approachable and an interesting alternative for mezcal, bacanora, and sotol fans. This one is definitely one of my favorites.

Tasting Notes - JN
N: first note is almost meaty, very sweet smoke, aromas from a teriyaki and honey marinated beef jerky, there is still some baked apple in the distance, barberries.
P: obvious smoky but not at all meaty, more like a campfire, some salty spots, very clean and dry.
F: the smokiness is increasing, it gets drier, the finish lasts very long, no fruitiness left.
C: first I expected to drink a smoked ham, but was surprised how dry and purely smoky the whiskey turned out to be on the palate.

ALMOND WOOD
Prunus dulcis

Almond chips

Ripe almond

Description
The almond tree is a small, deciduous tree native to Asia and the Middle East that is related to the peach tree. When it comes to alcohol, most people associate almonds with Amaretto, an Italian liqueur flavored with almonds. However, the whiskey made from smoked almond tree wood is quite unusual and striking.

Almond wood gives a mild and slightly nutty taste that is good for a wide variety of uses. It is most often compared to pecan wood. It is far milder than woods like mesquite and hickory. The nose is quite mild, with all the smoke coming out near the finish on this batch.

Tasting Notes - NF
Nose: Intensely fruity like smoked apples, but also floral, such as the pollen of certain varieties of lilies. The smoke is a gentler than the alder wood sample.

Palate: The lily and floral notes are not as present on the palate, and the fruit also dissipates. There is more smoke on the palate, but it is a dry smoke. It is a bit like liquid smoke.

Finish: Mid-length, dry smoke finish.

Tasting Notes - JN
N: very fruity like a piece of pear in a cigar box, fresh and greenish, plum pit, not too much smoke, buttery like ghee.
P: obviously smoky, but dry and slightly phenolic like a cold chimney, freshly ground black pepper.
F: heats up the mouth and becomes appley again, the finish lasts middle long.
C: a very pleasant whiskey with a high drinkability which is not dominant in any direction!

APPLE WOOD
Malus domestica

Apple chips

Apples ripening on the tree

Description
Apple wood is a familiar smell to many people, as it is used to smoke bacon and many other meats. Like most fruit woods it has a pleasant sweetness to the nose and is milder than many other hardwoods. Its pleasant and comforting aromas make it a real standout among all woods for smoking; however it can be weak on the finish, and needs to be paired with something else for a well rounded whiskey.

Tasting Notes - NF
Nose: Smoky nail varnish, very sweet fruit. A little tropical, with mango.
Palate: Surprisingly very spicy, with chipotle and cayenne peppers predominating. Lots of sweet mango chutney with chipotle peppers.
Finish: The smoke is still sweet, with a mid-length finish.
Conclusion: A very interesting combination of Indian mango chutney with Mexican chipotle peppers. It would certainly be an interesting culinary experience for the organoleptically adventurous whiskey drinker out there.

Tasting Notes - JN
N: nothing of the expected apple aroma, maybe some passion fruit and sweet banana in the distance; but quite meaty, roasted hazel- and beechnuts, wet tobacco leaves, spicy like juniper berries.
P: dry and still meaty, a bit like a long dried black forest ham, quite sweet.
F: the sweetness lingers very long as the black forest ham aroma does.
C: May I have some dark bread and butter, please?

APRICOT WOOD
Prunus armeniaca

Apricot wood chips

Fresh Apricots

Description
Apricot wood smoke creates a whiskey with great finish, but is weaker on the nose than other fruit woods. The finish is long and pleasant. This fruit wood has more floral elements than most fruit woods making it more complex, but weaker in terms of overall smokiness. The signature apricot smell is sadly absent, but the finish is noteworthy and wonderful.

Tasting Notes - NF
N: Very fruity, but with a hint of shoe polish.
P: Has a bit of a tanned leather quality; quite smoky, with a nutty quality that is much like a roasted New Mexico pinon nut.
F: Quite a long finish of fire-roasted New Mexico pinon nuts.
C: Interesting finish, not what I would expect from apricot.

Tasting Notes - JN
N: cold smoke, slightly fruity like pineapple, mint, honeydew melon with prosciutto, tonka bean, a bit earthy, some sweet caramel.
P: again sweet-fruity like tinned pineapple with syrup, but much smokier on the palate, roasted pine nuts and cashews, a bit oily, mouth coating.
F: after a short heating effect the taste dries out and leaves not too much sweetness, the palate-coating oiliness sticks very long.
C: I expected apricot aromas, juicy and sweet, and if the apricot wood is not offering that particular flavour I hoped for at least getting some almond aromas, but nothing at all! OK, I must admit, it did not meet my expectation, but was it disappointing instead? No way! Imagine a chilly autumn evening, the sun is to going to set and the leaves seem to glow in bright colors! This is the perfect moment for a whiskey like this!

ASH WOOD
Fraxinus americana

Flowering Ash tree

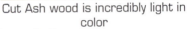
Cut Ash wood is incredibly light in color

Description
Ash trees are actually a genus, Fraxinus, that contains about 50 species of medium to large trees. They are related to lilac and olive trees. It's great for firewood and is used as a smoking wood for barbecue. North American White Ash is what I used in these experiments.

Tasting Notes - NF
Nose: Mild smoke, with a lot of baked apple and pear with caramelized sugar; a hint of rubber and sulfur, pungent.

Palate: Surprisingly sweet on the palate, with toasted hazelnut. Browned butter, and very little spice. The sweetness is like a type of smoked salmon called "Indian candy."

Finish: Long but the smoke is milder than on many of the samples.

Tasting Notes - JN
N: sweet and creamy, green walnuts, some honey-kind smokiness, thick and sticky, grainy like a freshly harvested field, sun heated hay.
P: dry and clean, freshly burnt wood, cocoa powder, forest honey, slightly phenolic.
F: First very clean but after a while it gets some treacly sulfury notes, becomes oily. There is a certain warming effect on the palate that lasts very long.
C: In contrast to the smell the taste is very clean, dry und straightforward, almost dusty. If not knowing better, I could just estimate where the ASH tree got its name from!

AVOCADO WOOD
Persea americana

Avocado wood chips

Ripe avocado

Description
Native to Central Mexico, avocado is a relative to cinnamon and bay laurel. They have been cultivated for at least 10,000 years for their avocado fruit, which is technically a berry.

Tasting Notes - NF
Nose: First impression is very sweet and citrusy, like orange blossom honey. It smells like the bees have a hive near an outdoor fireplace.

Palate: The sweet honey translates to the palate. Lots of orange citrus, too, could be orange blossom or perhaps candied orange peel.

Finish: Sweet, long, and citrusy, with very dry smoke.

Conclusion: There is an interesting but curious counterpoint between the sweetness of the orange blossom honey and the dry smokiness, but there is no organoleptic dissonance from this relationship. Not what one would expect from avocado wood!

Tasting Notes - JN
N: very soft, like a sweet wine, not too much smoke, caramel, vanilla,
P: some sulphury smokiness, ripe fruit, still some sweet wine left, but not as dominant as on the nose. Caramel, vanilla, burnt wood
F: the sulphur sticks to the tongue but lowers. Aromas like roasted nuts evolve.
C: the smokiness developed after letting this whiskey breath. In the beginning it seemed to be not at all smoky but after a while a broad, thick smokiness came through.

BEECH WOOD
Fagus sylvatica

Beechwood smoked malt

Beechwood logs

Description
Beech trees are large deciduous hardwoods native to North America, Europe, and Asia. Beechwood works well as a firewood and has a long history in beer production. Beechwood is smoked to produce smoked malt and it is also used as a fining agent. The beech smoke is key to the flavor of traditional German Rauchbier.

Tasting Notes - NF
Nose: Very light smoke, if any at all. There is a lot of fruit, such as ripe banana and pineapple on the nose, along with butterscotch and toffee. Underneath the sweet fruit there is also a dry earthiness.

Palate: Black pepper spiciness that was not there on the nose now shows up, also some dried fig, caramelized banana, and toffee. There is some initial heat on the palate that later smooths out.

Finish: Short finish, with a whiff of gentle smoke now coming onto the palate, but no depth.

Conclusion: Very approachable for those that might not prefer the bold smoky whiskeys.

Tasting Notes - JN
N: not too smoky, caramel and cookies, almonds, milk chocolate with nuts and raisins, pear, some floral aromas like violet and freesia.
P: very dry smoky, close to coal, but not very intense, clean and straight forward, nutty, winey.
F: middle long, the clean smoke lingers.
C: After nosing I expected something opulent and was surprised how dry and lean this whiskey is. The taste is great with a high drinkability.

BIRCH WOOD
Betula cordifolia

Description
Birch trees are deciduous hardwoods related to beech, oak, and alder trees. They are widespread throughout the northern hemisphere. The signature birch bark is white and silvery. It is prized as a firewood because it burns without popping and even when wet due to the oils it contains.

Tasting Notes-NF
Nose: Gentle smoke on the palate, and has much of the same dried fig and toffee.

Palate: Same dried fig and toffee as on the nose, but the smoke really comes through on the palate. Interestingly, the smoke has a "creaminess" about it.

Finish: Mid-length, semi-sweet smoky finish.

Conclusion: This is a very approachable, yet lightly smoked dram.

Tasting Notes - JN
N: sweet smoke but obviously fruity, baked apple, banana, vanilla, creamy, leathery.
P: unexpected peppery, again sweet smoke, dried fruits like apple and banana chips, a bit medicinal but not unpleasant, creamy like a caramel flan, vanilla.
F: it stays sweet for quite a long time and dries out slowly, gets more bitter.
C: this is a whiskey that sneaks in slowly. In the beginning I thought it is nothing special and the more I think about it, the more I like it. Pity, that my glass is empty…

Birch Wood

BLACK WALNUT WOOD
Juglans nigra

walnuts

Description
Black walnut is a deciduous, flowering tree native to North America. It is grown for its nuts and for its timber. Though less dense than oak, it gives a deep and rich smoke character when burned to malt. The big, rich, and meaty nose made this smoke flavor really stand out and it is a staff favorite at Corsair.

Tasting Notes - NF
Nose: Green walnut notes, with a brightness and pungent smoke. Also some spice, and has a smoked meat quality that is much like a hot coppa ham or some other type of smoked salumi.

Palate: The hot coppa ham and green walnut smoke predominates on the palate. There is an intense "meatiness" about this whiskey.

Finish: Long finish, with a very smoked salumi type of note.
Conclusion: Definitely not for the faint of heart or for vegetarians!

Tasting Notes - JN
N: obviously meaty, campfire smoke, phenolic, oily, raisins and dried apricot.
P: phenolic, cold and sticky smoke, earthy, peppery, very ripe fruits, sweet and dry.
F: very long, it sticks to the tongue and seems to stay forever.
C: Although the whiskey is very clean the taste is dirty like thick smoke.

CEDAR WOOD
Juniperus virginiana

Cedar kindling

Products made from cedar

Description
Cedar is a genus of medium sized evergreen coniferous trees native to the Himalayas. For my experiments, I was using Eastern Red Cedar, though a number of other cedars are common near me including Lebanon, Atlas, and Northern White cedar. It has a history in alcohol production as Japanese sake traditionally used barrels made of cedar. It is often used in cooking with cedar planks adding oils to meat cooked on them. Typically cedar, like pine and other softwoods, is not recommended for smoking. We went ahead and tried it anyway as I love the smell of cedar.

Tasting Notes-NF
Nose: Not surprisingly, lots of cedar notes, but also a maritime-like briny, oily note much like smoked salmon or mackerel. Lots of caramel, salt toffee, and pecan pie filling underneath the brine and salmon. One of my favorites.
Palate: In addition to the cedar and green oak notes, there is a surprising amount of pecan pie sweetness on the palate.
Finish: Sweetness fades back to briny, salty, maritime-like smoked salmon for a mid-length finish.
Conclusion: A very surprising but pleasant dram.

Tasting Notes - JN
N: Obviously smoky, like a cold chimney, but not too strong, woody aromas like a just sharpened pencil, some green apple and dusty cocoa powder.
P: The picture of the pencil comes again to my mind, but the smoke dominates slightly, there is not too much fruit left, just some apple in the distance. The taste is very straight forward and clean.
F: The wood shavings dominate and develop certain bitterness, middle long finish.
C: This was surprising! I expected from the cedar lots of spices, diffuse smoke and warm aromas, but it turned out to be a very clean whiskey, almost lean and cool.

CHERRY WOOD
Prunus avium

Description
Cherry trees have their origins in Asia and are now grown all over the world for the their fruit. The distinctive cherry flavor of the fruit comes through into the smoke. Cherry wood smoked malt is a malt we have worked with extensively at Corsair and is the backbone of our Triple Smoke and Nashville whiskeys. It pairs exceptionally well with other hardwoods in blended smoked whiskeys.

Tasting Notes-NF
Nose: Initial nosing has bold notes of Persian sour cherries, pomegranate syrup, and cranberry juice with lots of red berry sweet and sour aromas, with a hint of walnut. Again, for anyone familiar with Persian cuisine, it is a lot like the walnut-pomegranate sauce and chicken stew called Feseenjoon, or perhaps even Chinese sweet and sour pork. Very light smoke on the nose.
Palate: Again, the same sweet and sour cherries and pomegranate notes, with a hint of toasted walnut.
Finish: The smoke tends to come out more on the mid-length finish, but the red cranberry-sour cherry-pomegranate notes are still present.
Conclusion: A most curious and intriguing dram that could easily be enjoyed by those with a taste for sweet and sour.

Tasting Notes - JN
N: Sweet-sour and the cherries cannot be overseen. Nothing what I would call smoky. Like an overripe fruit cocktail. Next to the cherries some pineapples, pears and tangerines. Almost juicy.
P: Again sweet-sour but this time with a slightly phenolic punch (both meanings), very fruity and juicy, some tobacco leaves.
F: Gets more smoke in the aftertaste, the fruitiness disappears slowly.
C: I have never smoked, but I can imagine that a cigar, kept with a piece of pear in a box made from Spanish cedar, comes quite close.

COFFEE WOOD
Coffea arabica

Roasted coffee beans

Description
Coffee is a genus of flowering trees grown for their seeds, mistakenly called coffee beans. The caffeine in the coffee plant is a natural defense mechanism to keep insects from eating the plant. Although many woods do not transmit the flavor associated with the tree, coffee wood, when burned, imparts an amazing coffee aroma and flavor that when mashed and distilled makes it all the way to the final whiskey, making this a most fascinating smoked whiskey.

Tasting Notes - NF
N: Lots of initial campfire smoke, but once the smoke has cleared, it paves the way for some delicious dark chocolate, kabobs with red pepper, purple onion, meat and pineapple cooked over a not charcoal grill, then come the smoked peppers, candied ginger, toasted marshmallow, and toffee.
P: The first palate entry has an enormous amount of pepper spice and wildfire smoke….wow! Just as suddenly, a huge wave of mint floods over the tongue and crashes against the back and sides of the palate.
F: The finish is mid-to-long, but not as long as I would have thought it would be for such a huge whiskey. Mint, chipotle pepper.
C: I never would have suspected this would be such a full flavored whiskey. I found it immensely enjoyable, and I wish I could have another!

Tasting Notes - JN
N: Thick, steaming smoke, roasted peanuts and pine nuts, but also a lot of sweet smoke like flambéed exotic fruit (orange, pineapple, mango), heat-cracked poppy seeds, also a bit meaty like a carefully smoked soft pork sausage.
P: Pork sausage again, this time flavoured with juniper, bay leaf and white pepper. I expected the smoke much stronger, but it steps aside to make way for the extremely peppery and floral notes of biting juniper. It even has a chilling effect on the tongue!
F: The floral note of the juniper disappears quite quickly, but the pepperiness stays. Suddenly there is also a lot of liquorice and fennel.
C: No matter if you like this whiskey or not, it is a fantastic example for a whiskey which has a lot going on. With so many surprising turns and twists it is anything but boring. Not knowing it better, I could have guessed it was made by Jan Fleming's Q - special effects guaranteed!

COTTONWOOD
Populus section Aigeiros

Description
Cottonwood trees are a type of poplar native to North America. They are very large deciduous trees with a very distinctive diamond shaped leaf, soft wood, and deeply fissured bark. The seeds have a distinct cottonlike structure they attach to that let the seeds be blown across large distances, for which the tree gets its name.

Sadly this was a very late addition. No third party taster could be used, but I did still want to include something about it as this a commercial smoked malt now available. This malt was not made and smoked by Corsair, but rather the Colorado Malting Company. Normally I do not include any company verbiage, but this was pretty funny and so I included it.

Maltsters Notes - Colorado Rauch Malt 2.0-2.5 L, (Colorado Smoked Malt)
Alamosa means "cottonwood." That's why we smoke our 100% local grains in 100% Colorado Cottonwood smoke. This grain is not only grown and malted in Colorado, but its also smoked with Colorado smoke! This smoked malt is bursting with smokey flavors and aroma. Be ready to make your smoked beer smile. "People in Colorado choose to smoke alot of different things. We choose to smoke malt."

Distilling Notes - Darek Bell
N: Pleasant mesquite like nose with hints of citrus. Dried fruit, raisins, burnt sugar.
B: Thick, white oak like smoke on the body.
F: Nice long burn, with good distant campfire and smoky meat finish.

C: Does not get too ashy or sulfury in the finish. In brewing this smoked malt the aroma was more subtle than other smoked malts. The final distillers beer became more pronounced. Distillation lost some of the flavor and we feared the barrel would take away the rest. It did for a while, then the smoke flavor came back after about 6 months in the barrel. The whiskey now has a nice smoke character similar to white oak, with no sweetness and without the ashiness. This was unexpected due to the soft wood. You can see a picture of the smoking apparatus the maltster used on page 57.

CRABAPPLE WOOD
Malus sylvestris

Ripe crabapples

Description
Crabapple trees are medium sized deciduous trees closely related to apples. They grow a small apple-like fruit that is much more sour than traditional apples. The trees are often grown as ornamentals and for their fruit. Like apple trees they have a sweet and pleasant smell similar to apple and pear trees, but are less distinctive than pears and milder than apple wood.

The smoked wood has a light, sweet flavor that is less sweet than fruit wood species. The sweetness keeps the smoke from becoming too bitter, resulting in a very clean flavor. It is less dense than other woods and therefore tends to have a lower chance of acrid and ashy off-flavors developing. Anyone enthusiastic about smoke should get to know this wood because it is so versatile. It makes an excellent "base" smoke that can get accents from other places or it can be used all by itself. This wood should be in everyone's toolkit whether you are interested in making whiskey, cocktails, or just want to grill some meat.

Tasting Notes-NF
Nose: Old leather, like a horse saddle or an old dusty book, earthy, sooty like a damp fireplace.
Palate: Lots of heat on palate entry, then soot and sweet smoke.
Finish: Sweet smoke at palate entry then turns a bit creamy with a long finish.
Conclusion: Interestingly, no apple on the nose or palate.

Tasting Notes - JN
N: First nose is cold smoke and vulcanized rubber, although it is not overwhelmingly strong. After a while there are also a few fruity aromas showing up like grapefruit and strawberries. It is a bit nutty with aromas from burned leather.
P: Smoked citrus notes, zesty and sweet, nutty and herbal.
F: the sweet smoke sticks to the tongue, middle long finish.
C: Where is the apple aroma? I expected at least a tiny bit of the bitter-sweet taste of a small, autochthonous apple.

GRAPE WOOD
Vitis vinifera

Grape wood branches

Grape vineyard

Description
Grapevines are part of a genus of flowering, vining plants grown for their grapes to be eaten or fermented into wine. Because the vines never grow as thick as trees, the wood never has the same thickness as other types and can be a hassle for smoking. This is offset by the excellent flavor and all around pleasantness of the final smoke flavor, which makes it a great blending or foundation smoke to build from.

Tasting Notes - NF
Nose: And it burns, burns, burns, this ring of fire (and smoke)! Oily and varnish-like, tropical fruit with black sooty smoke.

Palate: Quite intense on the palate, with a heavy phenolic, iodine flavor.

Finish: Long and phenolic.

Conclusion: Not as well balanced as I prefer. I enjoy smoky whiskeys, but this one seems to be reminiscent of licking a fireplace wall.

Tasting Notes - JN
N: Fruity smoke, sweet and meaty, vanilla, almost creamy, some nice Christmas spices.
P: While the nose is quite soft and sweet the taste hits you like a kick, very powerful and strong. Again quite sweet but the smoke is thick, almost oily and dominating, a bit phenolic.
F: there is an almost pungent bite that keeps very long.
C: This is one of the whiskeys that starts like a lullaby and turns out to be a thriller instead.

HAWAIIAN GUAVA WOOD
Psidium guajava

Wood chips

Guava fruit

Description
Guava trees are small, tropical fruit trees native to Central America and grown throughout the tropics and subtropics. The wood is used for meat smoking in Hawaii, Cuba, and Mexico. It is grown for its fruit, which has a distinctive aroma that does not come over in the smoke, but many other fruit and tropical aromas do. Like other fruit wood it has a pleasant smoke flavor.

Tasting Notes-NF
Nose: Good gentle smoke, with a fair amount of dark dried fruit as well as tropical fruit, such as toasted coconut and pineapple.

Palate: A hint of brown spice is on the palate entry, then the gentle smoke, sweet toasted coconut, and pineapple come rolling back, and a touch of vanilla crème pie.

Finish: The tropical fruit and dried dark fruit give way to a mid-length finish of dry smoke.

Conclusion: A most enjoyable and well-balanced whiskey. I'll have another, please!

Tasting Notes - JN
N: intense cold but sweet wood smoke, some fruity (apple) layers underneath. Although smoke usually turns out to be a bit dirty this whiskey smells very clean, nearly crisp. The smell reminds me of a burned piece of wood with a thick black crust.
P: Again the smoke is the most obvious but now it seems to come from coal with some coal dust.
F: Does coal taste bitter? The longer it stays in the mouth the more bitter it gets.
C: Reading "Guava" I expected something fruity, but apart from a hint of apple on the nose there is no fruit at all.

HAWAIIAN KIAWE WOOD
Prosopis pallida

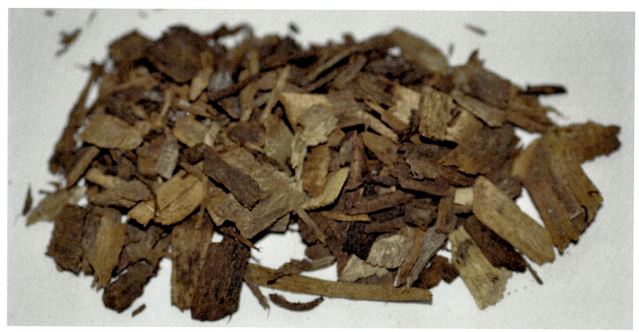
Kiawe wood chips

Description
Kiawe is a medium sized, bushy tree native to Central and South America.

Tasting Notes-NF
Nose: A minimal amount of smoke on the nose, with a rose potpourri top note; salt toffee.

Palate: The minimalist smoke on the nose comes out with a roar on the palate; salt toffee is still present, with some black cherry and cocoa notes behind that.

Finish: Short to mid-length in finish, and the roar of smoke slowly dissipates. Nicely balanced.

Conclusion: Like the other Hawaiian wood whiskey, this one is very pleasant.

Tasting Notes - JN
N: fruity smoke, some dried sweet prune and strawberry in the distance, like a chimney on a cold snowy day.
P: very phenolic, cold smoke, burned hazelnut, still some dried prune.
F: the phenolic taste lingers, gets more nutty.
C: The interplay between smoke and fruit is very exciting, pity that the finish is mostly phenolic and not that fruity anymore.

HAWAIIAN OHIA WOOD
Metrosideros polymorpha

Description
Ohia is part of the myrtle family of trees and can be found in all 6 of the largest Hawaiian islands. It can grow on lava rock and is sacred to Pele, the volcano goddess, in native Hawaiian traditions.

Tasting Notes-NF
Nose: Hay, polished leather, oil, savory aromas, light brown spice, with some toast and nut.

Palate: Polished leather predominates, but there is also some roasted hazelnut, pencil shavings, and cedar.

Finish: Lots of cedar, hazelnut, and pencil shaving ride on a mid-length wave, but then a smoky nutmeg and Jamaican allspice wave takes over.

Conclusion: The intense nutmeg finish was not expected, since it is not prominent in the nose or palate. A nice drinking whiskey with a surprise at every turn!

Tasting Notes - JN
N: My first impression: "spicy chimney," although I know that it is very difficult to describe, how a "spicy chimney" could smell. You might find such an odor in a tobacco or sausage factory, or in a combination of both. The spicy mixture contains pepper, chilli and vanilla.
P: The spice mixture is dominating the taste, too. It is sweet, hot, warming, oily, and all is held together by smoke.
F: The spice is stepping back and the smoke is dominating.
C: Even though this whiskey reminded me of a chilli sausage there are no meaty aromas like in a dried ham. It is more like a dry smoked sausage which you traditionally find in Austria and Switzerland.

HICKORY WOOD
Carya ovata

Description
Hickory is one of the most dominant smoking woods. While the flavor and aroma are not the most distinctive, this wood does provide a nice "distant campfire" aroma and makes a great base from which to bolster other smoke flavors and types.

Tasting Notes-NF
Nose: The aroma is one of, well…hickory!

Palate: For those who like barbecue, this whiskey has lots of smoked hickory short ribs notes, smothered with a tangy tomato sauce that is sweetened with thick molasses.

Finish: The tangy and sweet tomato based barbecue sauce turns to a slightly bitter liquid smoke.

Conclusion: This whiskey would pair well with a barbecue meal.

Tasting Notes - JN
N: Nutty, fruity (mainly citrus aromas and pears), dusty smoke, burned potatoes.
P: Cold campfire, nutty, quite phenolic and mineralic, again burned potatoes.
F: The campfire seems to be fanned up and is glowing again.
C: What intrigues me in one moment, disgusts me within the next. It seems that I cannot make up my mind about this version.

JAMAICAN PIMENTO WOOD
Pimenta dioica

Description
Pimento trees are native to Central America and grown all over the world for allspice. Allspice is made from the undried fruit of the pimento tree and derived its name from having flavor characteristics of cinnamon, nutmeg, and cloves. Allspice is especially important to Caribbean jerk seasoning. It is also a key component in Middle Eastern stews. When the wood is smoked it creates a bold smoke with spicy, herbal, and medicinal notes.

Tasting Notes-NF
Nose: Intense sweet smoke, a hint of nail polish, grilled pineapple, pepperoni, and other salamis

Palate: Campfire smoke, then a very bright, fruity taste with pepperoni predominating. Tastes much like a Hawaiian style pepperoni and pineapple pizza.

Finish: Short to mid-length with fading smoked meat

Conclusion: Another intriguing combination of flavors, creating an exciting jazz-like trio of smoke, meat, and tropical fruit.

Tasting Notes - JN
N: Sweet and spicy, warm smoke, dried fruits, some herbs.
P: Spices! Spices! Spices! Not as sweet anymore as on the nose, but the dried fruits and the herbs make the taste complex and nice. The smoke turns out to be a bit medicinal.
F: A dusty woody smoke dominates the spices but the finish is still warm and mouth-filling.
C: This is exactly what I've expected! The well combined spices and herbs together with the warm smoke make this whiskey very complex and tasteful.

LEMON WOOD
Citrus limon

Lemon wood

Description
The lemon tree is a small evergreen tree originally from Asia and grown for its citrus fruit. The sour and tart taste and smell of the lemon fruit makes it a key ingredient in food, candy, cocktails, desserts, and a number of beauty products. The wood has an intense yellow color and citrusy smell. When burned it creates a thick oily smoke unlike most other woods. When malt is smoked with lemon wood and made into whiskey it has a number of interesting traits of the lemon. The distinct citrus smell is imparted and an oily finish changes the mouthfeel of the final spirit. It makes for a fascinating smoked whiskey that tastes more like a gin than a whiskey.

Tasting Notes-NF
Nose: Lemon wood creates a totally unexpected organoleptic experience of dry hay, autumn leaves, brazil nut, and pan-roasted pine nut.

Palate: The palate is extremely dry and spicy, with a strong hay and grass taste.

Finish: Dry, dry, dry with a slightly bitter lemon rind, smoky hay finish.

Conclusion: Where is the lemon? I would have imagined there would be some lemon in the nose or palate.

Tasting Notes - JN
N: Freshly baked cookies, peppery smoke, spices like cinnamon and nutmeg, and yes, there are also some citrus notes but more zesty than fresh and juicy.
P: Very spicy and dry, peppery cold smoke, very dark cocoa powder, roasted nuts.
F: Very long, the smoke sticks to the tongue, gets bitter and a bit oily.
C: Another whiskey that turns back my expectations regarding fruit or floral aromas – but in a very positive way. It is very surprising and whenever I take a sip, it always offers me new impressions. Pity, that my sample is empty now.

LILAC WOOD
Syringa vulgaris

Description
Lilac is a type of large flowering, deciduous shrub related to olives. It is native to the Balkans and grown all over the world as an ornamental. It is known for its sweet smelling flowers that make it popular in parks and gardens.

Tasting Notes - NF
Nose: Intense smoke that is reminiscent of mesquite, lots of hay, leaves, and savory tarragon; wild agave, cranberry juice, guava.

Palate: Waves of mesquite, tarragon, white pepper, cinnamon stick, a hint of ground ginger, and wild agave roll over the palate.

Finish: Mid-length finish of tarragon and white pepper, with a rush of smoke and cinnamon evolving.

Conclusion: This is a well-balance whiskey, with a nice level of smoke. An overall pleasurable dram.

Tasting Notes - JN
N: Fresh and fruity, red berries, freshly ground pepper, cold smoke in a smokehouse, some estery notes like in fresh spirits

P: The smoke dominates the palate; burned wood and charcoal are the most obvious impressions. There is still some fruit and also pepper but not as multi-layered as on the nose.
F: The smoke gets drier and makes way to very dark chocolate aromas.
C: What seems to be a lightweight on the nose changes significantly on the palate. There are no blossoms, no wispy flavors, but the massive power of smoke and dark roast aromas.

MACADAMIA WOOD
Macadamia integrifolia

Description
Macadamia is a genus of nut trees native to Australia. Native Aborigines consumed the nuts for thousands of years before commercial cultivation. It is now grown all over the world for its edible nut and as an ornamental.

Tasting Notes - NF
Nose: A immediate pungent smoke hits the nose, then turns into newly polished leather, macadamia nut, smoked ham or salumi, tomato-based sweet barbecue sauce, with an underneath aroma of sour cherry.

Palate: Smoked ham, tree bark, macadamia nut, cedar chest, pencil shavings, and sweet barbecue sauce glide over the palate

Finish: Mid-length finish of sweet smoked ham fades to bitter cedar and more polished leather.

Conclusion: This whiskey reminds me of my grandmother's old cedar chest.

Tasting Notes - JN
N: Cold bonfire, burned hay and straw, a warm forest with humid ground during summertime, a bit meaty.
P: Cold ash of a coal fire, no meaty aromas anymore, very clean, nearly crisp, nearly no fruit apart from some ripe apple, a little bit of walnut.
F: Still clean and crisp, turns into cocoa powder.
C: Where is the nutty aroma? I hoped to find some typical macadamia nut, which I love to nibble in abundance to calm myself when watching a thriller. I doubt that this whiskey has the same effect, although it will probably help to maintain my weight.

MANUKA WOOD
Leptospermum scoparium

Description
Manuka trees are a type of flowering plant native to New Zealand and part of the myrtle family. They have been used for a number of purposes. The leaves were used for tea and made famous by Captain Cook. Manuka honey is cultivated when bees use manuka flowers for nectar. The wood is very hard, and makes a great flavor for fish and meats when smoked.

Tasting Notes-NF
N: Intense smoked meat, such as smoked ham or chicken; smoked Gouda cheese, cream.
P: The smoked Gouda cheese and general creaminess follow through to the palate. Waves of smoked ham flood over the Gouda to make a delicious "smoked ham and cheese" whiskey.
F: A short, dry smoked finish follows.
C: This whiskey would go very well as a smoked aperitif, coupled with smoked cheese and salami. The smoke is well balanced.

Tasting Notes - JN
N: Sweet wine, like a good Oloroso Sherry, ripe fruits like mango and sharon, honey glazed lamb shank, dry flower honey (I understand why bees like Manuka!), creamy, buttery, vanilla and caramel. Where is the smoke? It is nearly not detectable and covered by winey sweetness and meaty spots.
P: Hello smoke! Finally I found it, although it is not too strong. The smoke is dry and clean like charred staves of a fresh barrel. Again honey glazed meat. The sweetness of dessert wine and fruits plays again the dominant role. The whiskey is still creamy and buttery and reminds me a bit of crème brûlée.
F: Middle long, the winey sweetness lingers, but the smoke is fading away.
C: A great whiskey for those who don't like smoke monsters! The little smoke that shows up here is very well combined and contributes to a huge complexity. I could imagine having this whiskey as a pre-dinner drink instead of sherry which is taste-like not too far away. It gives you a good glimpse of what to expect on your plate – including dessert.

MANZANITA WOOD
Arctostaphylos manzanita

Description
This North American tree is known for the distinctive red and orange bark and winding branches. Although often used as a decorative, the berries and bark are edible. When the wood is used to smoke malt and then made into whiskey, the results are very unusual and distinctive. This unique wood has many chocolate and spicy notes. The nose is a little weak, but the body and finish have unique chocolate notes that blend well with other base smokes like white oak.

Tasting Notes-NF
Nose: Chocolate chip cookie dough, Play-Doh, black Mission fig balsamic vinegar drizzled over ripe cherries, grilled pineapple, Southern pecan pie and chocolate chips with Bourbon sauce, sticky sweet Pedro Ximenez sherry. Dessert in a glass!
Palate: Palate is somewhat drier than the nose, with some chocolate chip cookie dough and black mission fig balsamic vinegar drizzled over cherries remaining. The smoke comes through on the palate much more so than on the nose.
Finish: The finish is very much like a malt finished in sherry butts, with some dryness coming though short to mid-length.
Conclusion: Another very nice whiskey with lots of fun flavors to dazzle the palate.

Tasting Notes - JN
N: Cold smoke, a bit meaty, some zesty and caramelized citrus aromas, a bit oily, dark chocolate, roasted herbs.
P: A dry and dusty coal cellar with some shrivelled apples on the shelves, beautiful roast aromas, hay and herbs, dark chocolate, multi-layered and absolute enjoyable.
F: relatively short but very intense, only the dark chocolate lingers a bit longer.
C: It reminds me of some cold and foggy winter days in my childhood when visiting my grandparents in the GDR. I guess it was always so foggy because most of the families heated with coal. While I was not sure if I will really like this whiskey when nosing it, the taste was a great surprise and made me pour another glass (no spitting this time).

MAPLE WOOD
Acer saccharum

Maple wood chips

A maple leaf

Description
The smoke from maplewood creates one of the most distinctive whiskey flavors I have ever tried. The nose and body are pleasant and full of sweet smoke character. The finish is the most fascinating of all the hard woods I have tested. A pleasant maple sweetness comes out at the finish. At Corsair maple has become a favorite especially for blending with other types of smoke. The long pleasant, maple and pancake-like smoke finish makes this an exceptional wood for making whiskey.

Tasting Notes - NF
Nose: Pine nuts, thick maple syrup over cinnamon pancakes, pungent smoke.

Palate: The pine nuts and pungent smoke come out most prominently, with more polished leather; honey baked ham. The maple syrup over cinnamon pancakes makes a brief return performance on the palate.

Finish: Short to mid-length, with the honey baked ham and maple syrup turning to dryness and smokiness.

Conclusion: I was expecting the palate and finish to have more of the maple syrup over cinnamon pancakes instead of the dryness.

Tasting Notes - JN
N: Apple, banana, sour cherries, freshly burned wood like after charring the inside of a barrel in a cooperage.
P: Cognac-like, intense spicy wood aromas, bitter-sweet, some vanilla in the distance.
F: Very complex and wood-spicy, long and warming.
C: There are no smoky Cognacs but whenever someone will hit upon this idea I could imagine that it must taste like this. The very elegant note after French oak together with the unobtrusive smoke make this whiskey so exceptional.

MESQUITE
Prosopis alba

Mesquite chips

Mesquite beans

Description
The deciduous mesquite tree is found in the southwestern United States and northern Mexico. It is usually small and shrub sized though it can grow as high as 30 feet. It is most commonly found in arid and semi-arid lands and is very drought resistant. The wood burns very hot and slow, making it an ideal grilling wood that adds a distinctive flavor common in Southwest and Texas-style barbecue.

Tasting Notes - NF
Nose: Brazilian black beans with salted smoked meats (known as "Feijoada," the national dish of Brazil), wild desert sage honey, saddle soap, wax.

Palate: The same black beans and smoked meats as above, as well as some oiliness on the palate. The wild desert sage honey is on the initial palate entry, but then fades to saddle soap.

Finish: The beans and smoked meats, and sage honey notes turn increasing dry for a mid to long finish. A hint of bitterness pervades throughout.

Conclusion: This whiskey gives me a mental impression of being somewhere in the desert of the American southwest.

Tasting Notes - JN
N: Dry green and herbal notes, some chilli spiciness, passion fruit, diffuse smoke.
P: Quite phenolic and salty, cold and sticky peat fire, bitter orange, spicy, oily and mouth watering.
F: Mid long, intense and warming.
C: This whiskey reminded me of some really peaty Scotches. When nosing them, you are not able to detect the full peatiness, but it hits you like a hammer on the tongue.

MULBERRY WOOD
Morus rubra

Mulberry chips

Ripe mulberry fruit

Description
Mulberry trees are deciduous flowering trees known for their edible fruit widely used in jams, wines, cordials, and tea. The fruit has a distinctly tart flavor with red and black mulberry fruit being the strongest. Of the fruit woods we have tested, mulberry has an incredibly pleasant smoke flavor when malt is smoked with it and made into whiskey. The strength of the smoke and wonderful flavor make this a unique smoke flavor with incredible potential for whiskey and beer makers. Why has no one ever made whiskey with mulberry wood before?

Tasting Notes - NF
Nose: Bright smoke, antique varnish, wet eucalyptus leaves, menthol.

Palate: Wet eucalyptus and menthol coat the palate, dried oregano, then a wave of charred frankfurter rolls onto the palate.

Finish: A mid-length finish of charred frankfurter predominates, with a secondary wave of juniper berry coming through.

Conclusion: A curious whiskey that makes one ponder: eucalyptus with charred frankfurter?

Tasting Notes - JN
N: Nuts and almonds, winey, the smoke seems to be as sweet and thick as molasses.
P: Very clean and crisp, nearly slim, cold smoke, much drier than on the nose, diet raisins (if there is something like that).
F: Quite long and mid intense, peppery, one-dimensional smoky first, but it gets sweeter again.
C: I was looking forward to a Rum & Raisin kind of whiskey after nosing, but was disappointed then by its dryness. At second glance and after knowing what to expect I found this whiskey not that bad anymore and enjoyed the clean, cold smoke. It seems to be like in real life: this is good candidate for a late, mature love!

OREGON MYRTLE WOOD
Umbellularia californica

Description
The myrtle is a large hardwood native to the California coast and grows all the way to Oregon. Its leaves have an intense spicy smell reminiscent of bay leaves. Native Americans used it as a medicine for headaches. Its wood was used as a currency, myrtle wood coins, during the Great Depression in North Bend, Oregon.

Tasting Notes - JN(Only Julia's notes are available for this wood)
N: Peppery sweetness, slightly meaty and oily, overripe citrus-fruits with a caramelized crust, banana and overripe apple, warm spices.

P: Meaty smoke like a carefully roasted ham, cold campfire with glimmering spots and melting marsh mallows, again overripe fruit and dry wild honey.

F: The sweetness disappears quickly, the smoke gets a bit bitter and lingers.

C: Like the Manuka wood, which belongs also to the myrtle family, both smoked whiskeys have an obvious sweet note and a great complexity. It seems that Myrtle wood has a good and tasteful impact to such kind of whiskeys.

NECTARINE WOOD
Prunus persica

Nectarine chips

Nectarine fruit

Description
The nectarine tree is a deciduous fruit tree native to Asia. It is the same species as peach, but has a smooth fruit with orange flesh. The tree is also related to cherry and plum trees. When burned the smoke has a wonderfully sweet, pleasant flavor, but is less distinctive than some other fruit woods.

Tasting Notes - NF
Nose: Sweet honey, a kiss of candied orange peel, Medjool date syrup, brown sugar, marzipan, grilled figs over a campfire.
Palate: Medjool date syrup and orange citrus fades to a drier smoked salmon, briny note.
Finish: Mid-length finish with lots of smoked salmon.
Conclusion: Lovely sweetness on the nose. A very enjoyable whiskey.

Tasting Notes - JN
N: Very ripe fruits, nearly overripe strawberries lying on hay, slightly meaty, fresh dough, not more smoke than in any barbecue sauce, seems to be oily and dusty.
P: Far more smoke on the palate, obvious citrus aromas, again a bit dusty.
F: Warming, only cold smoke lingers in the end.
C: While the smell was quite sweet with all the ripe fruit aromas, the taste was a dry surprise. There must have been a big portion of barbecue sauce with some sour elements involved. Must be great to season some steaks!

OLIVE WOOD
Olea europaea

Olive tree bark

Ripe olives

Description
The whiskey made from olive smoked barley is truly unique for several reasons. The nose is herbal and vegetal in a way unlike almost all the other tree and wood-based smoke flavors. There is a gin-like quality and a pleasantness similar to the fruit woods, but at the same time unique and more memorable. The finish becomes oily, but remains pleasant and distinct.

Tasting Notes - NF
Nose: Green olives with rosemary and dried oregano, Meyer lemon, sage brush.
Palate: The green olives with rosemary and oregano are present but slightly muted. A dry smoke predominates with a hint of brine.
Finish: Mid-length smoky finish with cedar and oregano.
Conclusion: This whiskey would go well with an appetizer of olives.

Tasting Notes - JN
N: A sun heated olive grove with the residuals of last night's bonfire in its middle, quite herbal, some juniper.
P: Air dried Buendnerfleisch (a meat speciality from the Grisons canton in Switzerland) combined with the cold crackling of burned wood, some medicinal notes, very dry, sour cherries.
F: Middle long, is getting slightly bitter.
C: What reminded me of holidays in Greece and made me dream of a gin martini with an olive in the glass, lost all of its summer character on the tongue. I should rather think of having some warming liquid next to my fireplace, avoiding hail and snow outside.

ORANGE WOOD
Citrus sinensis

Orange wood chips

An orange tree full of oranges

Description
Orange trees are flowering, evergreen trees widely grown in tropical and subtropical climates for their signature sweet fruit. They are the most widely grown of the citrus fruits and the most important economically. The wood has a slight orange color that is very unusual. The wood smells citrusy and when burned creates a thick oily smoke. The resulting malt has an intense citrusy and oily smell to it that is wonderfully bizarre and memorable, making this one of the most unique smoked whiskeys I have ever made.

Tasting Notes - NF
Nose: Intense candied orange soaked in tawny port, sweet pipe tobacco, gingerbread cookies, burnt sugar.

Palate: High ester Jamaican rum & allspice, ash, rope tar, with some dried orange citrus underneath. The gingerbread is a bit muted on the palate, but is still present.
Finish: The candied orange and tawny port dry out to a tarry, mid-length pipe tobacco finish.
Conclusion: There are many surprises in this whiskey, from fruity Jamaican rum to tawny port! It is good to see the orange aromas in the smoked orange wood. I am quite fond of this whiskey.

Tasting Notes - JN
N: Bitter orange zests, thick and oily, burned caramel, vanilla, bittersweet.
P: Spicy smoke, slightly bitter, mouth filling, dry, slightly phenolic.
F: The smoke steps back, the bitterness is growing, still phenolic.
C: Why do I think of Crême brulée? It must be that blend of aromas that makes my mouth watering. If there is a Chef reading this and is picking up my idea, please name it after me: Julia's funky Crême brulée! It will make you a superstar!

PEACH WOOD
Prunus persica

Peaches in the tree

Ripe peaches

Description
The peach tree is a deciduous fruit tree native to Asia and related to cherry and plums trees. It is known for the juicy, fuzzy fruit it bears. The smoke has a sweet, pleasant flavor, but is less distinctive than some other fruit woods like mulberry or pear.

Tasting Notes - NF
Nose: A big aromatic helping of cobbler with ripe summer peaches, cinnamon & dark brown sugar crust! Somewhat similar to the Orange Wood whiskey in that there are also notes of gingerbread cookie.
Palate: The peach cobbler returns to the palate, but there are also some red berry notes hidden underneath the brown sugar cinnamon crust. The smoke comes in gentle waves after the cobbler goes down the gullet.
Finish: Light smoke, with some notes of peach and cinnamon. The finish fades away softly.
Conclusion: Another approachable whiskey that is a delight to savor.

Tasting Notes - JN
N: Ripe fruit, thick sweet wine – Marsala-like, nutty, cinnamon, some tar in the distance.
P: Still sweet but far more tar, creamy like soft fudge, very complex and spicy, ripe lime.
F: Regardless of its softness it is quite long, also one of the few finishes that is staying sweet, gets some herbal aromas.
C: Wow! This is stunning! The aromas seem to play with my taste buds. One moment I could swear this whiskey is smoky, the next moment it seems to be spicy, and then the sweetness is knocking on my brain asking for attention. I should name it "discussion whiskey" because it talks to me!

PEAR WOOD
Prunus persica

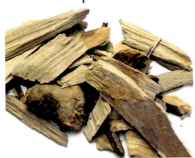
Pear chips

Pear fruit

Description
Pear trees are a flowering, mostly deciduous group of fruit bearing shrubs and trees native to Europe and North Africa. The wood has a pleasant pear and apple smell to it. When burned, the pear wood makes by far the most pleasant and distinguished smoke of the fruit woods. Mulberry is more intense, but pear has the best of the sweetness common to all fruit woods and makes a fantastic smoked whiskey in nose, body, and finish. Like other fruit woods it benefits from blending with a hardwood like oak or hickory to add more body to the final smoked whiskey. This is one wood anyone interested in smoked whiskeys should explore.

Tasting Notes - NF
Nose: Intense sweet smoke, tar, ash, charred oak, and campfire. Like the peat whiskey, this one has notes of smoked Gouda, but it also has some almond butter and caramel crème brulee.
Palate: The smoked Gouda stays on the palate, but then wave upon wave of ash and tar.
Finish: Smoked Gouda on wheat crackers trailing off into the sunset.
Conclusion: Where is the pear? This whiskey goes to show that the smoked wood from fruit-yielding trees does not necessary give off fruit-like flavors. I was expecting some fruit on the nose and palate, but there is none to be found. Except for the initial almond butter and caramel crème brulee on the nose, the sweetness dries out.

Tasting Notes - JN

N: Acidic smoke, wet paint, rotten hay, smoked ham.
P: Very dry smoke, nearly dusty, roasted nuts and almonds, spicy, mustard seeds, phenolic, prickling.
F: Middle long, peppery, still phenolic, the roasted aromas dominate.
C: I guess it was obvious that I didn't like the smell but the taste reconciled me. In the beginning my taste buds struggled a bit with the massive roast aromas, but the prickly effect made it quite pleasant.

PECAN WOOD
Carya illinoinensis

Pecan chips

Pecan nuts ripening

Description
Pecan trees are very large deciduous trees native to the Southern United States. They are a type of hickory tree in the Carya genus. They're known for their nut, the pecan, which is technically not a nut but a drupe, or fruit with a single stone pit. The rich buttery nuts are common in Southern cooking and New Orleans Cajun cuisine. When the wood is smoked it is similar to hickory, but less intense and more balanced.

Tasting Notes - NF
Nose: Unlike the pear wood whiskey, which tasted nothing like pear, the pecan wood smoked whiskey has a big burst of candied pecans! Unbelievable! There are strong, dessert-like aromas of pecan pie, pecan praline, dark honey, and salt toffee.
Palate: Sweet campfire with smoked honey-baked ham cooking away, then a big helping of pecan pie and dark honey sneak in afterward.
Finish: Mid to long finish with lots of honey baked ham and pecan pie lingering until the very end.
Conclusion: This whiskey was everything I thought it would be, and more. It noses and tastes like both dinner and dessert, a complete "meal" for any whiskey fan!

Tasting Notes - JN
N: Citrus fruits, white smoke, a bit phenolic, spicy after long pepper, nutmeg and cinnamon, banana bread with pecan nuts.
P: White smoke, again very spicy mainly peppery, now with some peppermint freshness, green walnut, coffee with pecan syrup.
F: Smoke and spices, it warms all the way down the throat till the tummy.
C: The spices are very intriguing; they make this whiskey so rich and complex. While I was sampling this, a picture of "Bannoffee pie" occurred to my inner eye. I once had this and it was topped with pecan nuts. Although this whiskey is not as sweet as this calorie bomb made of bananas, cream and toffee, it is as close as possible.

PERSIMMON WOOD
Diospyros virginiana

Persimmon wood

Persimmon fruit

Description
Persimmon trees are medium size fruit trees that produce an edible, sweet fruit. They are grown all over the world and can withstand a varied number of climates and conditions. They are quite hardy aganst disease and pest and are important to wildlife due to their trait of dropping fruit late into the winter.

Tasting Notes - NF
Nose: Fortunately, another whiskey whose wood is reminiscent of its fruit! Light smoke, with persimmon bread, nutmeg, cinnamon, allspice, pumpkin custard, candied yams, and cinnamon roll with sugar icing on top.
Palate: All the sweet fall and winter fruit dries out, but the brown spices such as nutmeg and allspice persist and become even more pronounced. There is some light smoke underneath, which is well balanced and serves to give the whiskey some nice complexity.
Finish: Mid length finish in which the brown spices fade into a trail of light smoke.
Conclusion: This would make an excellent holiday or fall and winter dram to enjoy by the fireplace!

Tasting Notes - JN

Nose: Fruity, slightly cheesy, Indian spices, nearly no smoke, in total quite shy.
Palate: Spices, spices and even more spices! Laurel, thyme, juniper and cooked ginger, quite peppery even with some chilli, warm smoke, juicy and mouth watering.
Finish: The mouth watering effect keeps you busy; the spices are fading away slowly.
Conclusion: I had quite some difficulties to name a few fruits which are showing up on the nose, but the smell is definitely fruity. On the palate the spices increase and leave nearly no space for anything else. I felt like being caught in a spice rack – what a nice feeling!

PLUM WOOD
Prunus americana

Plum wood chips

Ripe plum fruit

Description
Plum trees are fruit trees grown all over the world. They are believed to be the oldest fruit trees to be domesticated. They are relatives of the peach, nectarine, and almond. They are all considered "drupes," fruits that have a hard stone pit surrounding their seeds.

Tasting Notes - NF
Nose: Smoked ham and salami with black peppercorns, toasted black walnut, antique leather, with a hint of plum tart and burnt sugar.
Palate: Initial palate entry has much more baked plum tart and stewed fruit than on the nose, but that disappears as more of the black peppercorn salami makes its presence known on the palate.
Finish: The intense black peppercorn salami and plum tart fades into a long finish with the bitter burnt sugar becoming more pronounced.
Conclusion: A nice whiskey, but it would be nicer if the bitter burnt sugar finish would exit the stage a bit sooner than it does.

Tasting Notes -JN

Nose: Cooked plum, carefully spiced with cinnamon and nutmeg, sour-sweet red berries, green hazelnuts, slightly peppery, dark gravy, a hint of smoke.
Palate: Heavily spiced plum jam and dried prunes, still some sweetness, flambéed and caramelized red berries, roasted nuts, smoked ham, grind bark, cocoa powder.
Finish: Quite long and spicy, the fruity notes are the first to disappear.
Conclusion: I guess this was the first of all samples where I really found immediately what was written on the label. It must be a fantastic Christmas whiskey and I can also imagine pouring something to the mixture of plums, figs, dates and raisins that go into a fruit cake.

RED OAK
Quercus rubra

Red oak chunks

Description
Red oak is quite different than its white oak relative when it comes to flavor. Red oak wood is much less dense than white oak. It has a pimento and spicy character that is quite unusual and similar to the Jamaican pimento tree smoked whiskey.

Tasting Notes - NF
Nose: Unanticipated notes of tropical fruits such as guava, juicy pineapple, and overripe banana, and shaved coconut, along with orange peel and English plum pudding.
Palate: The unctuous tropical fruits and orange peel persist, but the sweet smoke, raisins, black currant, dried dates, figs, and plum pudding taking over.
Finish: A light, but smokey, sweet finish with lots of candied dark fruit.
Conclusion: Another good whiskey for fans who prefer their whiskey on the sweet side. Who knew red oak would produce such a sweet, fruity whiskey?

Tasting Notes - JN
N: Sweet wine-like, ripe fruit, biscuity, warm spices, a bit peppery, caramel and vanilla, just a hint of smoke.
P: White smoke, spicy, peppery, citrus aromas, slightly meaty, fresh almonds.
F: Middle long and warming, develops some cocoa aromas towards the end.
C: I would call this whiskey "roller coaster" but it has nothing to do with the equally named Scottish bottling from Islay. It reminds me of a kind of a fun fair long gone, with music from different booths, the hubbub of many people talking and laughing, caramelized sweets and grilled sausages. You can smell it all in one time, but you can also smell the brakes of the roller coaster going hot. Very enjoyable!

SASSAFRAS WOOD
Sassafras albidum

Sassafras chips

Description
Sassafras trees are large deciduous trees native to the United States and Asia. The flavor of the roots is most commonly known in traditional root beer, but were also used in perfumes, soaps, and food. Most commercial root beer today is synthetically flavored. This is because safrole, a chemical in sassafras, is believed to be a carcinogen and was banned in 1960. I am including my research here because I personally would rather try a natural substance used by humans for thousands of years than a chemical that is less than 60 years old. However, do not expect the federal TTB to approve a sassafras smoked whiskey if you choose to make one.

Tasting Notes - NF
Nose: A root beer float with vanilla ice cream in a whiskey glass! Savory and spicy aromas with a sweet undertone predominate. Lots of licorice, anise seed, candied ginger, black peppercorn, and smoky sweet tomato-based barbecue sauce aromas.
Palate: The palate is very similar to the nose, with intense root beer, black licorice, and smoked barbecue short ribs on the palate.
Finish: A mid to long length root beer finish.
Conclusion: Very nice! A root beer float for whiskey lovers! It also reminds me of taking a walk in the woods and smelling sweet sassafras bark.

Tasting Notes - JN

N: Dry and cold smoke, earthy, sweetness from dried fruits such as plums and figs, a variety of spices, some tannins.
P: Thick smoke, burned pine seeds, intense spices mainly cinnamon and liquorice, resin, sweetness from overripe fruits, oily, some tar.
F: Very long and spicy, the thick smoke sticks in every taste bud and can hardly be washed away.
C: I can imagine that the oracle in ancient Greek's Olympia needed exactly this melange of aromas to fall in trance. But does it mean that I will be able to look into the future after having another sip? It is worth a try!

WHITE OAK
Quercus alba

Wood and acorns

acorns

Description
White oak contributes so much to a whiskey's flavor in the aging process because most whiskey barrels are made of white oak. What most distillers may not know is how much this wood, when smoked, can contribute to a whiskey's flavor. White oak smoke is a great base smoke. It delivers an intense and pleasant smoke character, especially in the body of the spirit. The nose and finish can be a little weak so it will need to be blended with other smoke flavors. It is a great smoke flavor to build a blend on.

Tasting Notes - NF
Nose: Very clean wood smoke, with toffee, browned butter, cinnamon toast with maple syrup, milk chocolate, candied walnuts, but then some pinenut and resin seep in.
Palate: Toffee, milk chocolate, maple syrup, and ash turn to resin and cinnamon toast.
Finish: Short to mid-length finish trails off with lots of smoke, ash, and cocoa butter.
Conclusion: A good, all-purpose smoked whiskey that would work well as an introduction to smoked whiskeys.

Tasting Notes - JN
N: Floral smoke like burned heather, leathery, herbal hay, roasted nuts, dried figs and raisins, the smell is not very intense.
P: First very dry but then a sweet smoke is coming through, roasted to burned nuts, still some herbal notes but nothing floral anymore, peppery.
F: The sweet smoke is getting dry again, middle long and peppery, the outside of the tongue is slowly getting numb.
C: Hmmm... I was expecting vanilla! But there IS no vanilla! Here in Europe there is always the same kind of "head-ballet": you mention "American white oak" to a group of whisk(e)y lovers and they all start nodding and muttering "vanilla!" Because this is the main aroma they expect from American white oak. And you see, I am not free of this, either!
OK, I try to flip the switch in my head and ask me again: Do I like it? Well... yes and no! The herbal aromas are intriguing, but I miss the interplay of flavors to make it a great drink.

BARRELS

Another distiller asked if we had ever smoked malt by burning whiskey barrels themselves. We liked this idea and immediately experimented with different types of barrels. We actually call this the oak category as they are all made from the same wood species Quercus Alba. Oak is a fantastic base smoke for building a smoked whiskey around. It is strong in the body, but weak in the nose and finish. Oak is an amazing sponge and really absorbs the flavors of whatever has been stored in it. Wine barrels add great character to the nose of the malt and final whiskey. Tabasco®, is a type of Louisiana pepper sauce that is actually barrel aged for two years in oak barrels. Amazingly, the Tabasco® character really comes through, making a striking spicy smoked whiskey with a peppery nose and a long spicy finish.

In the future I would like to take a spiced rum barrel, a cognac barrel, and a barrel aged gin barrel, smoke grain with those and see what kinds of whiskey come's from smoking the malt with those barrel types.

BOURBON BARREL

Description
Someone asked me, "Why not smoke grain with Bourbon barrels?" So we did and boy am I glad. We had a lot of extra barrels and the resulting smoke was wonderful and clean, with intense toffee and caramel notes. My whole garage smelled like heaven for a week.

Tasting Notes - NF
N: This whiskey offers lots of caramel sweetness, as well as toasty, charred, smoky, spicy and fruity aromas. There is also a fair amount of pipe tobacco, pecan pie filling, allspice, cinnamon, and overripe mango.
P: The spiciness that was initially on the nose takes front seat, with the smoke and fireplace ash tailing a close second. The peppery spiciness on this whiskey is so aggressive that my tongue started burning mid-palate.
F: The hot pepper subsides into a long, dry, smoky finish.
C: Yet another unsuspecting whiskey. I was greatly surprised that the palate had the degree of hot spice, as in pepper spice, that it does, since the kind of spice on the nose is more toward the brown spice family.

Tasting Notes - JN
N: Cold ashy smoke with some sweet fruit wine in the distance, a bit meaty like fresh pork sausage, ripe pear and dried spices.
P: Wow! This is like biting in a freshly charred barrel while it is still hot! The smoke is not too dominant anymore but the spiciness and also some sulfury notes take over the lead. There is a vital chilli aroma that burns down the throat but, fortunately, goes not too far.
F: The finish is middle long but it is warming and gives you another spicy kick.
C: Yet another surprise whiskey! The smell and the taste are so different and totally unforeseen. It reminded me of Indonesian dishes I once had in Amsterdam. Unfortunately someone forgot to put the icon for "hot and very spicy" in the menu and the ingredients were written in the original language. It was an unforgettable tasting experience that affected my tongue for three days!

CABERNET BARREL WOOD

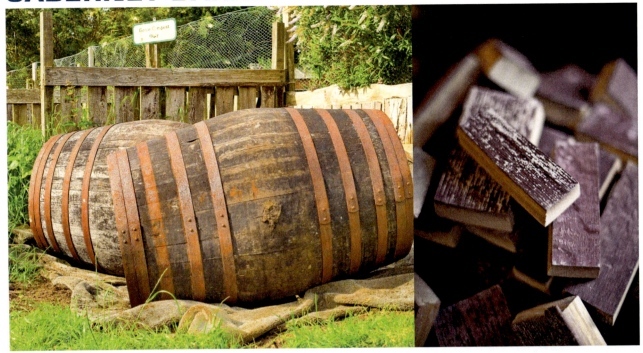

Description
I love the deep purple color of this wood. When burned it is has less oily residue than the other barrel types. The red wine smell comes out strong on burning and is incredibly intense. it just goes to show you what an amazing sponge oak is for soaking up flavors of the spirit that was held.

Tasting Notes - NF
Nose: Nice wine and red berry notes with gentle smoke predominate.
Palate: Echoes of black red cherry roasted over a fire; currant liqueur mixed with a drop of liquid smoke; faint burned rubber (sulfur candle?).
Finish: Gentle smoke with the black currant syrup.
Conclusion: Well balanced dram, good tension between the red berry and smoke.

Tasting Notes - JN
N: Although a smoky note comes first, the wine cannot be ignored. The smoke is like a just blown out candle, a bit waxy and it seems to disappear quickly. Baked apple, slightly spiced and plain chocolate with chilli.
P: Again the winey note is obvious and it softens the smoke, makes it sweeter. The smoke seems to be a bit stronger than on the nose, earthy and dusty, again chocolate but this time without the spice chili character.
F: A bit sulfury in the aftertaste, maybe the barrel was sulfured or just the wine, but still sweet and fruity, middle long.
C: The wine does a great job, gives some sweetness to the whisky and softens it. Very pleasant!

FRENCH OAK BARREL

Description
This wood smelled incredible when I opened the package. Upon smoking it made for an incredibly fruit filled smoke smell.

Tasting Notes - NF
Nose: Very dry smoke, autumn leaves burning, oatmeal cookie with raisins, and lots of berry fruit, such as cherry, blackberry, and raspberry.

Palate: Lots more smoke from burning leaves, with some overripe blackberry and intense black peppercorn spiciness.

Finish: There is smoke of course, but the finish has a very curious biscuity, barley malt, and bran-type of finish. The sweet berry fruit completely disappears at this stage, leaving only the dryness.

Conclusion: Since there did not appear to be much spice on the nose, I was surprised to find so much black peppercorn on the palate.

Tasting Notes - JN
N: cold smoke, quite spicy and herbal with a honey sweetness, some oat flakes and warm dust in a summery barn. I expected some winey notes but there aren't any.
P: Again cold smoke joined by hay and herbal spices. There is a nice but not too strong sweetness of honey and vanilla which softens the smoke. Again some cereals, mainly oat and wheat flakes.
F: Middle long, the sweetness dries out and makes way for the smoke again.
C: If you expected French opulence you might be disappointed. If not, you will be delighted by a middle smoky, grainy and soft whiskey with a nice sweetish appearance, something to enjoy as pre-dinner drink!

TABASCO® BARREL

Description
When I heard that Tabasco® sauce was aged in oak barrels, I just had to get my hands on some of the wood and see what it was like when smoked. A thick, nasty smoke came off when burned and it made my eyes water. It was a brutal smelling smoke and left a lot of oily black residue. I expected this to be the nastiest thing ever, and in some ways it was, but it started to grow on me though I am not a fan of spicy foods.

Tasting Notes - NF
N: Spicy, but the nose is quite sweet, like barbecue sauce slathered over tender pork ribs; spicy Mexican chorizo and salsa; red beans and rice with smoked sausage and Tabasco® sauce slathered on top. Upon later passes, a hint of toasted coconut comes through.
P: The barbecue sweetness turns into an amazingly spicy pepper hot, hot, hot dram! There is also some tang on the palate.
F: The finish is mid-length, but the spicy pepper subsides as the sweet ketchup and honey-based barbecue sauce makes another appearance.
C: The Tabasco® barrel smoked whiskey reminds me of the type of cuisine from the states of Texas and Louisiana. There are barbecue and Tex-Mex flavors, smoky sausage notes, and lots of big, bold flavors to be found all the way from the nose to the finish. This whiskey just doesn't quit!

Tasting Notes - JN
N: Smoked toffee, vanilla, some biting spices prickle in the nose, nutmeg and cinnamon, also curry, burned hay.
P: Hot mouthfeel, quite spicy, again softening toffee, mint and chili.
F: Quite hot, becomes a bit sulphury and herbal before it calms down.
C: My expectations were hot! Only reading the word "Tabasco®" made me think of a spicy and maybe even burning whiskey. But the result was so-so. Quite spicy on one hand with chili aromas and a heating effect, but on the other hand I found softening toffee and vanilla that calmed down the whole thing and made it easy drinking. But anyway, in my opinion this whiskey is neither fish nor fowl and it cannot make a decision where it belongs to.

ROOTS & BARKS

I read that the Native Americans did not just use tobacco, but would mix a number of herbs, roots, and barks in with tobacco for smoking purposes. In the next section the items were smoked dry and used in the same proportions as the woods for smoking.

BAYBERRY ROOT

Description
Bayberry has been a symbol of good luck and fortune for centuries. The tree grows near swamps, marshes, or water in sandy soils. The leaves have a pleasant fragrance that has been used commercially in candle making. The roots are used in teas and tinctures, and have been used medicinally as an anti fever, antibiotic, and as an astringent.

Tasting Notes - JN
N: Sweet-sour berries like red currant and gooseberry, bitter citrus aromas like lime zests, quite fresh and even grassy (which disappears quickly).

P: Middle strong smoke of young wood, still a bit green-ish and bark dominant, fresh hey, pickled vegetables, bitter herbs like wormwood.

F: The fresh vibrant style changes quite quickly into a mouth coating bitterness, which disappears slowly and leaves the impression of a medicine.

C: I am not yet sure if I like this whiskey or not. Firstly the nose intrigued me a lot because it was so lively and fresh, but the taste became medicinal and bitter and therefore not so enjoyable.
BTW - I just see that Bayberry Root is also used as homoeopathic medication for liver damage. May I ask you to send me an extra bottle? .. just in case!

BIRCH BARK

Description
Birch trees are deciduous hardwoods related to beech and oak trees. Birch bark peels easily from the tree, but is slow to decay, making it incredibly useful to Native Americans for building materials, as paper for writing, for containers, and making canoes. When burned for smoking grain it results in a whiskey with a unique sandalwood like taste.

Tasting Notes - NF
N: This whiskey retains some of the "creaminess" of the birch wood whiskey, as well as dried black Mission fig, dried date, black currant, and black pepper. There are also hints of incense.
P: The cream has definitely exited to be replaced by a microscopic "gritty" mouthfeel, followed by lots of juniper, black peppercorn, dried orange bergamot, thyme, and rosemary. There is still some sandalwood incense lurking about. Are you sure this isn't a juniper heavy gin?
F: Mid-length and juniper heavy, with the sandalwood persisting.
C: This is yet another curious whiskey that starts out as a whiskey and finishes as a gin. However, the sandalwood incense aroma gives this dram a note which is quite unlike gin or whiskey, but very nice.

Tasting Notes - JN
N: Dusty cold smoke and ash, incense, burned fir twig, a sulphuric sweetness like some wines have, hay.
P: Lots of incense, ashy dryness, dried herbs, perfumed like dried blossoms, resinous like coniferous wood, big and intense.
F: It is getting ever drier and develops some oiliness at the back of the tongue.
C: This whiskey immediately reminded me of a huge catholic cathedral. When you enter it, there is mainly darkness and you are overwhelmed by the smell of incense. And as soon as your eyes are used to the twilight and your nose is adjusted to the damp smell you are overwhelmed by the size and the opulence of decoration... and depending on your personal experience you like it or not. It is the same with this whiskey! I wouldn't call this is a holy whiskey but it seems to have some skeletons in the closet crypt.

BLACKBERRY ROOT

Description
Blackberry bushes are perennial plants grown all over the world for their berries. All parts of the blackberry have been used as food and medicinally for thousands of years.

Tasting Notes
N: If I reach, I can pick up some blueberry or blackberry aromas, but also there are notes of smoked salmon and green capers. A second and third pass reveals sweeter notes of pecan pie, chocolate chip cookie dough, and salted caramel pudding.

P: Another helping of smoked salmon with briny green capers, chipotle pepper, and salted caramel pudding. The blueberry aromas are not to be found on the palate- were they just a figment of my imagination or are they real?

F: Short, dry finish of smoked salmon.

C: After drinking this whiskey, I am craving bagels, lox, and capers, followed by some pecan pie. This whiskey delivers a meal in a glass!

BUTTERNUT BARK

Description
The butternut tree is a deciduous tree related to the walnut tree. Butternut bark has been used medicinally to treat a number of maladies such as dysentery, smallpox, and other ailments.

Tasting Notes - NF
N: Wow, this whiskey smells like butternut squash with maple syrup drizzled on top- licked by the flames of a smoky grill of course! And don't forget the pumpkin pie with brown sugar on top. There are even "s'mores"-like notes of marshmallows with milk chocolate & graham crackers roasting over a campfire. However, a second pass or two reveals more campfire smoke than sweet aromas on the nose.
P: The palate is somewhat drier than the sweet squash notes on the nose. It is somewhat reminiscent of liquid smoke, but then toasted marshmallow makes a delicate return to the palate.
F: The campfire smoke lingers for several minutes.
C: This makes for a very pleasant drinking whiskey, and is very much dessert-like.

Tasting Notes - JN
N: Quite shy on the nose (compared with some of the other smoke monsters), quite sweet and nutty. fresh dough and cookies, tender sweet smoke, caramelized almonds, zests of grapefruit and kumquat
P: Thick smoke, first dry than sweeter, herbal, bitter almond, roasted hazelnut.
F: Very long with a bitter-sweet wave, meaning sweetness and dry bitterness alternate for a while.
C: Guess I have the same problem as the whiskey. I am indecisive! The whiskey seems to be like the weather in April and plays the good guy/bad guy game. And depending on which side of its face is shown, I like it or not!

CASCARA BARK
Description
Cascara is a tree related to buckthorn and native to North America. It was traditionally used medicinally as a laxative. Cascara has been used as a flavoring agent in ice cream, spirits, and pastries. Cascara is one of the most striking smoke flavors when burned. It tastes amazing, however I urge caution due to its medicinal history. This is one my favorites of the bark group.

Tasting Notes - NF
N: Intense aromas of saddle leather, smoky honey baked ham, shoe polish, Polish kielbasa sausage, sweet mango salsa with chili flakes and fire-roasted red pepper.
P: Wow, lots of heat! Hot, hot, hot coppa salami with black peppercorns, Tabasco® sauce, ground chipotle peppers over warm tortillas. Fruit-like notes such as mango and pineapple are buried underneath all the smoky peppers.
F: More pepper and smoke, but then a bit of sweetness kicks in for a mid-length finish.
C: Based upon the smoked meat aromas on the nose, I was thoroughly unprepared for- but pleasantly surprised by- the level of chili pepper heat this whiskey has on the palate. It would pair beautifully with authentic Mexican street vendor tacos and a good spicy salsa. What a fun whiskey!

Tasting Notes - JN
N: Fresh exotic fruit cocktail, just a hint of smoke, some honey, peppery spices, light as a fino sherry.
P: One sip and the whisky lost its lightness! It is now full of thick smoke, slightly meaty, very peppery and it bursts of intensity. What was sweet on the nose is now savory on the tongue!
F: The peppery spiciness lingers and has a heating effect down to the stomach.
C: This is a very good example that you should never evaluate a whiskey only by nosing. What seemed to be a lightweight and a spring whiskey first turned out to be a real winter warmer with a huge complexity. And therefore you should never trust a Scottish master blender telling you that he only creates his blends by smelling and never tastes. Believe me, he does!! .. and these people can withstand a lot of alcohol!

CATUABA BARK

Description
This flowering tree from the Amazon is used for a variety of purposes. It is used as an antibacterial but is most famously known as an aphrodisiac. When grain is smoked with catuaba and made into a whiskey, the resulting spirit has a pleasant smoke character, especially on the nose, but is not distinct enough to be used as the only smoke source. It works well when blended with other smoke types.

Tasting Notes - NF
N: Initial aromas reveal orange & tangerine citrus notes. These quickly turn to oysters in a smoked paprika sauce, with liquid smoke.
P: Layers of liquid smoke roll across the palate, covering any initial aromas of orange citrus. The oysters have faded, only to be left with smoked paprika and liquid smoke.
F: Short to mid-length finish followed by liquid smoke.
C: Aromatically, this is a strange whiskey, with a curious combination of citrus and oysters with smoked paprika.

Tasting Notes - JN
N: A funny mixture of overripe fruit and stale water, on one hand fresh fruity, citrus-zest-oily and green, on the other hand oxidised and somewhat dull, like a fruit wine which has been in an open bottle for days.
P: Not as oxidised as on the nose, this note has more or less been replaced by coal smoke. Still a lot of ripe fruit and oily citrus zests, some burned herbs and fermented tea leafs.
F: The fruitiness is disappearing while the smoke takes over and dries out.
C: Probably not one of my favorites! I always struggle with whiskeys which are quite good on one side and show a big "but" on the other side. The same here: nice fruity aromas, but... also oxidised and fermented ones. Even the promised aphrodisiac effect of the Catuaba bark is secondary for me.

FRINGE TREE BARK

Description

Fringe tree is a small tree native to North America with large leaves similar to a magnolia. The flowers have a white fringe like cotton. The bark has been used medicinally as a tea for liver ailments. When grain is smoked with fringe tree and then made into whiskey, the resulting spirit has herbal and pine notes.

Tasting Notes - NF

N: The nose is big, bright and fruity, with bursts of candied orange citrus, cherry, mango, dried date, and pineapple- very much like a smoky holiday fruitcake! There are notes of tawny port, stewed prunes, and blackstrap molasses.

P: The fruit is still present but muted. Soon after initial palate entry, heat and wood smoke overwhelm the fruit and the whiskey becomes too unidimensional.

F: The finish is surprisingly short and dry, given the initial "big" aromas.

C: The nose is very pleasant and has a lot of complexity, but I find this does not translate to the palate. It would be nice if the fruitcake notes were present.

JAMAICAN DOGWOOD BARK

Description
Dogwood is a tropical shrub native to the West Indies and the Americas. It contains a strong sedative that is not poisonous to humans. West Indian fishermen used to fill a box with its branches and put it in water. Fish would swim through it and fall asleep, making them easy to catch. The whiskey made from dogwood smoked malt produced strong bourbon-like notes that made me think this would complement a bourbon base wonderfully.

Tasting Notes - NF
N: Initial nosing revealed a reticent aroma, but upon a few swirls of whiskey in the glass, a big wave of smoke pops out of the glass and into your nose! Once the shockwave is over, the whiskey has aromas of honey sweet smoke that interestingly become slightly bitter, with charred oak and tar.
P: Campfire, tarry rope, ash, iodine, and medicinal, with blackstrap molasses underneath and a curious taste of celery seeds that comes through after initial palate entry.
F: The finish is mid- to long, with more iodine and tar fading away, with hints of celery seed.
C: This whiskey reminds me of an Islay or maritime-influenced Scottish malt whiskey, but with a different kind of smoke source than peat. It is big and bold, with lots of intense smoke.

Tasting Notes - JN
N: Quite floral after pouring, but it disappears when breathing, stale water, cold wood fire smoke (increases with breathing), some burned rubber, bitter orange peel and quince.
P: The smoke is the strongest aroma; it covers some bitter herbs and salty caramel.
F: The smoke slowly disappears and makes way for a herbal bitter note and the remnants of some fruity sweetness, quite long.
C: A bit too bitter and one-dimensional for my taste, but I can imagine that a smoke freak could fall in love with it.

MUIRA PUAMA BARK

Description
One of the most flavorful and pleasant smoked whiskeys we have made at Corsair of the bark group is Muira Puama. The tree is native to South America and is known for its white flowers with a strong jasmine scent. The smoke it creates is rich with spicy Caribbean flavors that are strongly balanced between the nose, body, and finish. This bark creates an incredibly wonderful smoke character that anyone wanting to make unique smoked whiskeys should study.

Tasting Notes - NF
N: Lots of grilled tropical fruit aromas, such as pineapple, mango, papaya, guava, and banana, along with brown sugar and molasses.

P: The palate is even more interesting than the nose! An initial wave of the same grilled tropical fruit flitters over the palate, followed by Jamaican jerk spice rub (nutmeg, allspice, peppers, garlic, cinnamon, and thyme).

F: The sweetness of the fruit subsides to a mid-length finish of the allspice, peppers, and the savory thyme.

C: This is a fun whiskey, with lots of tropical aromas. Nice for a day at the beach!

PRICKLY ASH BARK

Description
This tree has a long history of use in Chinese medicine. The bark and fruit of the tree have been used to treat abdominal pain and as an anesthetic.

Tasting Notes - NF
N: This is one of the most intense, overbearingly smoky whiskeys I have ever nosed. The smoke is sweet to the point of being cloying. Notes of charred pineapple, burning leaves & rubbish, sugar cured ham, and habanera chili.
P: Initial palate entry is extremely hot & smoky in every sense: habanera chili, white pepper, slow-cooked pork over a smoky spit, shoe polish, antique leather.
F: The finish is true to form for such an intense whiskey, with an exceedingly long finish.
C: This is one of the few smoked whiskeys that is not to my liking. It is really quite a monster, with the burnt leaves, habanera chili, and shoe polish notes predominating. It left my head spinning and seems nearly toxic!

Tasting Notes - JN
N: Furniture polish, waxy, quite chemical and medicinal, flamed citrus peel, the smoke is not from a standard source like coal, peat or wood, it is more like burned plastic
P: The smoke is now much stronger but still plastic-like, some ash, the mouth feel is more of prickly chili than of prickly ash, the whiskey is quite dry and also a bit meaty
F: The chili prickles on and on and makes a very warm mouthfeel
C: This whiskey is very unusual and I think there aren't too many people liking it. The burned plastic note is not very pleasant and gives the whiskey a very artificial taste. It reminded me of a major fire in an industrial estate with toxic fumes.

QUASSIA BARK

Description
This South American deciduous tree's name is synonymous with the word bitter. It is the primary bittering agent used in many spirits, medicines, and in cocktail bitters. Insects do not touch the bark, leaves, or roots of the tree and it is commonly ground up and used as a natural substance for repelling insects. When burned to smoke malt the bittering agents are mostly left absent and the smoked whiskey produced is quite pleasing.

Tasting Notes
N: Desert sage, polished leather, smoked salmon, candied tangerine, hay, black mission fig, currants.

P: Dry smoke with lots of polished leather, smoked salmon, and a hint of black fig.

F: Short finish, but very dry with lingering smoke

C: Upon initial nosing and tasting, this whiskey does not seem to have as much aromatic complexity as some of the other smoked whiskeys. However, it opens up to reveal more dark, dried fruit.

WHITE WILLOW BARK

Description
Willow is a deciduous tree with long hanging leaves used by Native Americans medicinally. It is used in modern medicine as it contains salicin, a precursor to aspirin.

Tasting Notes - NF
N: There is something almost subtle about the first impression of this whiskey- vanilla bean ice cream, sea salt toffee, and green tree bark, but then comes a healthy dose of white balsamic vinegar and ash.
P: Any initial subtlety on the nose is now overcome with burned newspaper ash, stale cigarette butt, followed by the white balsamic vinegar. The smoky ash is exceedingly dry.
F: Short, dry finish of ash and vinegar.
C: This whiskey becomes more intense as the ashy aromas open up in the glass. It is a strange combination of flavors.

Tasting Notes - JN
N: Sweet smoke, very fruity like pear and ripe grapes, carefully smoked ham with Chinese sweet-sour sauce.
P: Sweet wine matured in a charred barrel with some extra burned staves. The second sip is much drier and lets the smoke come through much stronger, quite peppery, even astringent.
F: Very dry and towards the end quite bitter.
C: The more time I spent with this whiskey the more reluctant it was. Not in a way that it was mellower or less intensive. The whiskey was rather reticent and did not open up to tell me its story. Guess we won't become a couple…

YOHIMBE BARK

Description
Yohimbe is an evergreen tree native to Africa. It has been used medicinally as a tincture, tea, and pumice. It is commonly known as an aphrodisiac and sexual enhancer for men. It is also used as a stimulant and for natural weight loss, but these effects do not seem to come through in the final whiskey when malt if smoked with yohimbe.

Tasting Notes - NF
N: Barbecue pulled pork with a sweet glaze, sage honey, piles of leaves burning on a crisp autumn day. A second pass reveals a crispy cinnamon pastry with brown sugar icing.
P: This whiskey is literally dripping with a smoky, molasses-like sweetness- very barbecue-like, meaty, and tender to the bone! The palate is more savory than dessert-like, as the cinnamon pastry aroma is not as prominent.
F: Like the nose and initial palate entry, the finish retains those sweet smoky notes.
C: This whiskey brings back fond memories of growing up in the American South, with delicious aromas of slow cooked barbecue wafting through the air.

Tasting Notes - JN
N: Thick sweet smoke like in a tobacco shed, crispy pork crackling after hours in the oven, caramelized brown sugar with some vanilla spots, fresh cookies
P: Heavily smoked sausages, barbecue sauce, both have different smoke aromas and make it taste "double-smoked", green walnuts with skin, slightly bitter caramel
F: The meatiness disappears, the bitterness of the caramel increases, dark cocoa powder
C: When nosing I expected something mellow, easy drinkable and found a "double-smoked" aroma-monster on my tongue. But is this a reason to be disappointed? No! It was rather a pleasant surprise! Not just for the summer month, but it does a great warming job during wintertime.

HERBS

ANGELICA

Description
Angelica is the European cousin of the more familiar dong-quai. A graceful flowering plant related to carrots, dill, and fennel. The plant has a sweet aroma more similar to carrots than dill or fennel.

Tasting Notes - NF
N: Smoked celery root, earthiness, and hay, with overripe Bing cherry, raspberry, and blueberry.
P: Very smoky and earthy, with lots of root and tuber notes such as raw turnip; also a hint of bitter celery seed comes through. The Bing cherry and berries on the nose subside substantially on the palate.
F: The smoke subsides a little to leave a mid-length, earthy, hay-like finish.
C: This particular whiskey is quite earthy and dry.

Tasting Notes - JN
N: Dense middle-strong smoke, ripe fruits mainly mango and pear, cocoa powder, spicy, some nuttiness
P: Phenolic cold smoke, peppery and spicy, roasted nuts and again cocoa powder.
F: Long and warming, quite oily.
C: The thick smoke is more or less overpowering everything else and makes it difficult to find more subtle aromas of fruit and nuts. That's why this whiskey comes out quite one-dimensional – a must have for smoke freaks!

ANISE

Description
Anise is an herb with a strong licorice aroma and flavor. It is a member of the family that includes dill, cumin, fennel, cilantro, carrots, and caraway. Anise is one of the primary flavors in the spirit absinthe. When smoked the licorice character is very minimal and a lot of vegetal and medicinal notes come through.

Tasting Notes -NF
N: Smoked decayed vegetal matter, burnt hay, sweet licorice, soap, smoked salmon, salted caramel pudding, browned butter with burnt cinnamon.
P: Whereas the nose has more vegetal notes, the sweet licorice comes through strongly on the palate. There is also a good amount of spice- both brown spice and pepper varieties, such as allspice and white pepper. The sweetness of the licorice turns bitter.
F: A mid-length, smoky, bitter finish.
C: This makes for a unique dram whose aromatics and flavors are all over the map. It is certainly not what one might expect from anise.

Tasting Notes -JN
N: Dry, cold smoke with some medicinal notes, nice citrus aromas, but there is also some sweetness from caramelized fruit, fresh and lively.
P: Although the taste is a bit more phenolic this whiskey arrives at the tongue as lively and fresh as on the nose. It is even prickly.
F: Still phenolic, but a lot of sweetness softens the finish.
C: I expected something Gin-ish or Aquavit-like, but was surprised of the very individual character of this whiskey. Its liveliness makes it so pleasant and drinkable…and no matter how often you have a sip, you'll always find something new and interesting.

CALAMUS ROOT

Description
Calamus is a semi-aquatic plant that grows in marshes and near water with a long tradition of medicinal use in China and India. Its strong sweet flavors have been used to make fragrances and has been used as a substitute for ginger, cinnamon, and nutmeg. When smoked it has strong diversity of flavors and is great for adding flavor complexity to a whiskey. In blending it pairs nicely with some of the denser hardwoods.

Tasting Notes -DB
Sadly this one could not get to my judges so i had to wing it myself.

N: Spicy, mesquite like nose. Herbal and cayenne nose.
P: Black pepper, wild game meat. Distant campfire, but with a bit of smoking green wood and pine needles. Sage smoke.
F: Long ashy burn turns quite phenolic. The mesquite like spicy smoke character last all the way through the finish. Leaving a slight medicinal iodine character, though not like a scotch.
C: When I first smelled it I was afraid it would turn petroleum bad smoke on the finish, however it stayed pleasant. It is distinctive but not as much as cascara and without the smoothness of some of the others.

CATNIP

Description
Catnip is an herbaceous perennial grown all over the world. It is best known as being loved by cats, but what is less known is that it is closely related to mint. When smoked it is weaker in terms of flavors than the other mint family herbs, but it is possibly more useful to a smoked whiskey maker, as it extends the finish with an oilyness yet has fairly neutral flavor. If one was blending it with another strongly flavored smoke, like maple wood, the finish could be extended and amplified even further.

Tasting Notes -NF
N: Intense herbaceous and floral aromas, with mint and grass. The smoke is relatively light, but has a lot of ash qualities.
P: The herbaceous quality is ever present, but there is also some banana fruitiness as well. Black and red pepper spice show through after the initial wave of herbs, tropical fruit, and smoke.
F: The finish is relatively short, but gentle. The herbs make a brief appearance again.
C: I initially had some reservations about trying this whiskey, but was pleasantly surprised by it. It is a whiskey that is quite accessible, even to those who might not prefer smoked whiskeys.

Tasting Notes -JN
N: Sherry-sweetness, winey, just a hint of smoke, ripe fruit, caramel.
P: Cold, dusty smoke, nearly earthy, spicy, the sweetness is still there but not as obvious as on the nose, still some caramel and ripe fruit although the smoke tries to dominate.
F: Warm and nearly oily, a true winter warmer.
C: Catnip! The name seems to be so light, the smell was also sweet and light and made me expect something easy-drinkable, a kind of tralala-whiskey, something that doesn't harm your taste buds and washes down like a lemonade. But … eehm, no!! This was probably the misinterpretation of the year! My taste buds were shocked! Although in a friendly way! It just took them a few seconds to cope with the unexpected situation before they found out that there is no tralala but a lot of depth, warmth and complexity to enjoy! But I still doubt that my cat likes it!

CLOVE

Description

Clove buds have been used in food and medicine for centuries and were one of the first globally traded spices. Originally from the spice islands, or Maluku Islands in Indonesia, they are now cultivated worldwide. Some herbs can be faint in flavor; not this one. When smoked it is very intense and totally overpowers all other flavors. Even when blended, a tiny amount can dominate all other aromas. This is not for the faint of heart, but produces a wonderful smoked whiskey that is incredibly unique and flavorful.

Tasting Notes -NF

N: The name on this whiskey says it all: clove! While the smoked clove note rises above the other aromas, there is also a fair amount of other brown spice such as allspice, cinnamon, cardamom, and mace. I also detect some Seville orange marmalade bitterness, which complements the clove quite well.
P: The Seville orange marmalade with clove spiciness really shines through on the palate, followed by more allspice and cinnamon.
F: The orange marmalade fades into a drier bitter orange peel for a mid-length finish.
C: Overall, this is fun whiskey! It would go very well with orange marmalade.

Tasting Notes -JN

N: Cold, slightly phenolic smoke, nearly peaty, some ash, a soft floral note tries to make it's way, some sweetness in the distance.
P: Ash-like, phenolic, like a cold chimney, quite spicy with cinnamon, cloves and freshly ground long-pepper.
F: Full-bodied, peppery, spicy and warming, develops slightly bitter.
C: This whiskey is not for the faint-hearted! It's taste is very pungent and peppery. The intense smoke leaves no space for subtle flavors. I did expect it quite spicy and smoky, but not as strong and obvious as it turned out to be.

GINGER

Description
Ginger is a tropical perennial whose rhizome, or root, is the most common and widely used herbal remedy in the world. Ginger is one of the most important spices for food preparation in many cultures.

Tasting Notes - DB
This sample was not finished in time for my third party noses. I did the review myself.

N: Heinous off-flavors on the nose. Rotten eggs and burning diesel. BAD. Lots of sulfur.

P: The ginger actually comes through here, but only to burn the inside of your throat in a bad way. Mostly it tastes like how stale bong water smells.

F: The finish is all oily petroleum. It has a long kerosene like after taste that is far from pleasant.

C: This is by far the worst smoked whiskey I have ever had. It got all the bad off-notes of smoke but none of the good: petroleum smell, burning plastic, sulfury eggs. I almost pulled this spirit from the book but left it in as a cautionary tale for whiskey experimenters. Not even good for pickleback cocktails.

JASMINE

Description
Native to the Himalayas, Jasmine is a perennial climbing plant with sweet smelling flowers. It has long been used in religious and wedding ceremonies and is currently popular in the perfume industry.

Tasting Notes - NF
N: Ooh, nice! Floral, fresh, and sweet, like a French lavender soap; also has a touch of wood smoke for added measure. There is also some date and dried fig, making the nose somewhat reminiscent of whiskey matured in sherry casks.

P: The floral sweetness is prominent, with lots of black pepper and cayenne pepper following closely behind. There is also a mint-like quality that fills up the entire palate.

F: The floral, minty quality finishes fairly short, but then the wood smoke comes back for a second round.

C: Overall, I enjoy the jasmine notes, as they remind me of a spring day.

Tasting Notes - JN

N: A smoke house with some remaining sausages, cedar wood and citrus aromas, dried fruit, oily.

P: Peppery cold smoke, still a lot of citrus and dried fruit. I've never tried to bite into cedar wood, but it must taste like this.

F: The peppery smoke stays long and offers some bitter-sweetness towards the end.

C: Overall very enjoyable, although I expected something more fragrant and fragile. I especially liked the cedar wood here- or whatever it is that makes it smell and taste like cedar wood. It gives the whiskey a slightly perfumed but very fresh style and a high complexity.

LAVENDER

Description

Lavender is an aromatic perennial shrub that has been used since the time of the ancient Egyptians for its scent. It has been seen as promoting good health, improving mood, and even as an aphrodisiac. It is one of the most recognizable smells in the world. It is a key flavor of contemporary French cuisine.

Tasting Notes - NF

N: Wow, quite nice and floral! The predominant note is, course, lavender, but there are also notes of mint, chocolate, and dark cherries. The smoke is lighter and better balanced than many of the smoked whiskeys.

P: This whiskey boasts of mostly floral, lavender notes on the palate, but it is more like tasting a lavender scented soap. The soapiness really comes through on this one. The mint is still present, although the sweetness of the stone fruit and chocolate disappears.

F: There is an extremely long finish of lavender scented soap.

C: Even with the soapy quality, I enjoy the floral quality of this smoked whiskey. It reminds one of purple lavender blooming in the summer time.

Tasting Notes - JN

N: Very floral and winey sweet, liqueur-ish like umeshu, opulent ripe fruit like peach and plum.

P: Gosh! This is prickly and peppery! Lots of floral aromas (rose and violet) and again sweet-wine-like. There is also a small amount of smoke but very well integrated. The whiskey seems to be a bit perfumed which reminds me more of jasmine than of lavender.

F: Still prickly, the winey sweetness lingers and changes to bitter in the end.

C: This is like a rose garden. Next to each plant you find a lavender bush to keep away lice and moths. It does not only make a garden very colourful, but also fragrant like this whiskey.

LEMON BALM

Description

Lemon Balm is a perennial herb related to mint. The leaves have a lemony and minty smell. It is often used as a flavoring for ice cream, teas, candy, and candles. When burned for smoke they create one of the best flavors of the entire herb category. Whiskey smoked with this herb is fantastic, and unlike most of other herbs it is great when mixed with other smoke flavors, but can also completely stand on its own in the nose, palate, and finish of the whiskey.

Tasting Notes - NF

N: Lemon balm makes a very pleasant smoked whiskey with a full spectrum of aromas. The nose has quite a bit of lemon and citrus notes, fresh mowed grass, arugula, grilled pineapple, with herbs such as tarragon, oregano, and parsley. The smoke is fairly gentle and does not overpower the more gentle aromas. Very nice indeed!
P: All of the above notes follow through beautifully on the palate, except there is an unexpected wave of hot cayenne pepper spice.
F: The finish is mid-length, with lingering notes of red pepper and lemon rind.
C: All in all, a good smoked whiskey that is refreshing. This one would work well as a smoked whiskey aperitif.

Tasting Notes - JN

N: Delicate citrus aromas, the smoke is nearly hiding, subtle Christmas spices, some apple and cherry.
P: Again various citrus aromas carefully lifted with dry smoke, the warm spices calm down the freshness, but in an enjoyable way that results in more complexity. There are still fruit aromas but now dried figs and dates.
F: The spices play the most important role in the finish; they are nearly biting.
C: This whiskey matches great with chocolate. Just tried it with a middle dark one flavoured with orange oil. The funny thing is that the smoke disappears almost entirely.

LICORICE

Description

Licorice root is one of the oldest and most widely used medicinal herbs. It has an a strong history and usage in Chinese medicine. It is used as a flavoring agent in many products.

Tasting Notes - NF

N: Ooh, my first impression was that this is a very nice whiskey! The smoke is very gentle and nicely balanced. Sandalwood incense and meaty hot coppa salami take over upon first pass. Upon second and third pass, there is a sour, lactic type of note that begins to develop alongside the incense and salami.

P: Sandalwood incense, with cayenne and smoky chipotle pepper spice. Some of the lactic aromas on the nose carry over to the palate.

F: The sandalwood incense notes are persistent, and completely dominate the finish.

C: I initially enjoyed this whiskey, but as I spent more time with it, the sourness took over.

Tasting Notes - JN

N: Phenolic smoke, but not very intense, some burned rubber, bay leaf and turmeric, reluctant vanilla, bitter orange zests and hay.

P: Mainly spices, this time even joined by curry, green coriander powder and some chilli, the smoke is still not too strong but seems to be covered by wood.

F: Although the spiciness lingers long the whiskey turns into something odd and boring.

C: If this whiskey were a person I would assess him/her as an extrovert desperate for attention. First you are attracted and curious about the character, but as soon as you have a chance to look behind the facade you are getting bored and disgusted.

MINT

Description
Mints are not so much a plant as a group of plants in the Lamiaceae family. They are all aromatic perennial herbs that grow best in damp soil. Mint is one of the most used and recognized aromatic flavors in the world.

Tasting Notes - DB
Sadly, this one was not ready to send to the judges, I had to do the nosing on my own.

N: Dull, herbal vegetal notes. Green peppers and kale. A slight pineapple smell. Sadly no mint.

P: Peppery, hoppy, sharp spiciness on the body of the spirit. A cut tomato vine, but not the fruit, smell. I love hops, but here it does not work.

F: A hint of mint, but just fleeting. Slightly oily, but not as striking as many other herbs. This was less minty than many of the other mints I made. Puzzling.

C: Sadly this was a major disappointment. The smoke had a strong mint smell that was lost on the final whiskey. Nothing like the spearmint or the peppermint smoked whiskeys, which were really good and really unique.

MUGWORT

Description

Mugwort is an herb with a long history in beer making, but not in distillation or whiskey-making. It was used as a bittering agent before hops in brewing. It was believed in medieval times to protect one from evil spirits. When smoked it makes for strong bittering elements which are useful for balancing overly sweet smoke aromas(like cherry wood), but require a delicate hand as the bitter taste can quickly take over and negatively overwhelm the whiskey. Warning: this herb is seen by the federal government as potentially harmful.

Tasting Notes - NF

N: Just as one might expect from mugwort, the nose of this whiskey is both bitter and sweet; a touch of desert sage honey as well.
P: The palate leaves a bitter, incense-like taste, and notes of sandalwood. The sweetness of the sage honey completely disappears on the palate.
F: The finish is short, but very bitter and smoky, rather like gnawing on a stick of incense.
C: There is not a great deal of complexity to this whiskey, and the bitter smokiness definitely seems to predominate over the sweeter aromas.

Tasting Notes - JN

N: Soft coal smoke, slightly medicinal, chimneys on cold snowy days, dry herbs, roasted almonds (with skin, not sweet), dry cellar apple with some coal dust, caramel.
P: Very spicy smoke, some chilli, very peppery, heats the tongue immediately and therefore seems to be a bit medicinal.
F: The chilli aroma sticks oily to the tongue and keeps the warming effect.
C: This is whiskey with a kick! As ethereal as a mugwort syrup to relieve a cough! Need to keep the leftover for next winter to cure myself if necessary!

MULLEIN LEAF

Description
Mullein is a tall, flowering biennial from the Mediterranean that has been naturalized in North America. This pleasant and balanced smoke adds flavor complexity that is herbal and citrusy while still maintaining a pleasant distant campfire smoke aroma. The finish is pleasant, but not too strong. Blending with another smoke will beef up the finish.

Tasting Notes - NF
N: Sweet herbs, sage smudge, sweet grass, smoked ham, toasted graham cracker with a hint of orange citrus. Very light smoke, and well-balanced.
P: While the lovely aromatics of the nose do not come over as strongly on the palate, they are still quite present. The smoked ham makes more of an appearance mid-palate, but then quickly trails off to leave more of the sweet herbs and sage smudge.
F: Short finish, but a gentle, pleasant one.
C: Another enjoyable dram, which, with the sage smudge notes, is "spiritual" in more ways than one!

Tasting Notes - JN
N: Just a hint of smoke, very fruity, fresh and green like today's cut grass – not yet hay, citrus aromas mainly grapefruit, but also the sweetness of lime, some oiliness.
P: Again the oiliness of a glimmering fire, not as fruity anymore as on the nose, but still the warm grass/hay aromas with strong herbal and spicy spots, which keeps the whiskey fresh and refreshing!
F: Long and eucalyptus-like. It nearly widens the throat, stays spicy with a chilling effect.
C: Should I call it the "Australian whiskey"?? It is not only the eucalyptus style that makes me think of "Down Under," it is also the "upside down effect." This whiskey makes you awake if you are tired, it chills your throat when it is harsh and hot and it is also a careful refreshment for the whole body. Probably better than most pharmaceuticals! And the taste is better anyway!

OSHA

Description
The root of this traditional Native American herb adds a spicy and herbal smoke character to smoked malt. It was sometimes called 'bear herb' as it was observed that bears coming out of hibernation would eat it to stimulate appetite. The large roots have an intense celery smell to them. Although it is weak on its own, when mixed with other smoke types it can add flavor complexity especially to sweeter smoke flavors like fruit woods.

Tasting Notes - NF
N: Earthy and root-like; celery seed, with pungent shoe polish top notes; fresh wood shavings; pine, ground turmeric, cumin seed, hot curry powder, fennel. Oddly, very little smoke in this whiskey.
P: All of the above notes are intense on the palate, but the bitter celery seed and ground turmeric really shines through.
F: Long finish with lots of celery and turmeric, turning to an even more bitter end.
C: This whiskey tastes like a spice box! A couple of the spice notes truly overpower this whiskey, making it not as well balanced as it could be.

Tasting Notes - JN
N: Smoked celery and fennel, liquorice, green-ish herbal, peppery.
P: Again a lot of celery and fennel, even more white pepper and now also chili and lots of oriental spices. Surprisingly this whiskey has also a perfumed, nearly artificial note, it is quite biting and prickly, not very pleasant.
F: The celery gets in the lead and leaves a veggie-like greenish impression.
C: My first thought when nosing this whiskey was: "Where is the peanut butter?" because I love this children's snack. And to be honest, only a huge portion of crunchy, creamy peanut butter can make this whiskey enjoyable. The original taste is so pungent that you can hardly drink this whiskey neat. Guess we found the adult version of a popular dish! Eureka!

PEPPERMINT

Description
Peppermint is an herbaceous perennial plant native to Europe. It is a hybrid mint that is a cross between watermint and spearmint.

Tasting Notes - NF
N: Cool mint smothered with dark chocolate, rather like a York peppermint patty or Thin Mint Girl Scout cookie that has been cooked over a campfire.
P: The peppermint patty and chocolate mint Girl Scout cookie notes come out strongly.
F: A mid-length, cool, "take-your-breath-away" type of minty finish follows through.
C: This is a very pleasant and dessert-type of whiskey. Goes well with chocolate and mint.

Tasting Notes - JN
N: Where is the peppermint? Where is the smoke? Some shy smoke is showing up late and is not very intense, dry herbs like sage, basil and thyme, some hay.
P: A very clean smoke on the palate, nearly dusty, intense herb and alpine hay aromas, but not as much peppermint as expected, just a peppery spiciness, which makes this whiskey quite refreshing.
F: Fresh, clean and crisp, it could last a bit longer.
C: This could be the perfect whiskey for a long and lazy summer night. The aromas reflect a warm summer day which is cooled down with an evening breeze as soon as it gets darker. The wind disperses the wonderful herbal aroma from sunset watered gardens and the pollen from sun heated meadows. Although you can hear the fun and laughter of people having a BBQ in the neighborhood, you can only smell the fire but fortunately not the flat beer. This is how a smoky summer whiskey should be!

SAGE

Description
Sage is a perennial herb with a long history of medicinal, ceremonial, and culinary uses. In ancient times it was used to ward off evil. It has an intensely signature smoke. Very little material is needed to produce a lot of smoke, and lots of flavor.

Tasting Notes - JN

N: very spicy and ethereal, medicinal, slightly phenolic, resin, some mint and burned herbs,

P: again a mixture of smoke, burned herbs and resin as well as a mint freshness; very dry and slightly perfumed,

F: during the first part of the finish spices and resin dominate but they change towards perfumed hey, the ethereal mint gives a mouth-drying feeling

C: There are various aromas with this whiskey, but they don't interplay with each other. In summery I would say this whiskey is "quite interesting", but you know that "quite interesting" is the well behaving little brother of "sh..".

SKULLCAP

Description
Skullcap is a genus of flowering plants in the mint, or Lamiaceae, family. They are herbaceous plants mainly recognized by the shape of their flowers, which give them their name. Skullcap has a long history in herbal medicine.

Tasting Notes - NF
N: Mothballs, pungent bitter herbs, with a sickly lingering sweetness.

P: Bitter, smoky, ash-like, and generally unpleasant.

F: The bitter, ashy smokiness lingers long and is difficult to remove from the palate.

C: Unlike most of the other whiskeys, I spent very little time with this one because I found it to be so unpleasant, almost to the point of being repugnant. Definitely not a recommended smoked whiskey.

Tasting Notes - JN

N: The smell is a mixture of rotten plants with some perfume to cover the bad odour; also some stale water.

P: No, the taste is not much better! The perfumy note comes out even stronger.

F: I didn't expect a miracle (taste-wise) therefore I was not disappointed..

C: Here in Europe Skullcap is one of the "legal drugs" which is sometimes smoked instead of marijuana. Personally I have no experience with smoking or consuming drugs at all; I've not even had a single pull on a cigarette in my whole life. And to be honest: if something tastes like this, it is anything but tempting! I am absolutely fine with drinking smoked whiskeys because I know that there are much better ones than this!

SPEARMINT

Description
Spearmint is an herbaceous perennial plant native to Europe and Asia. It is a hybrid mint that is a cross between watermint and spearmint. Although so similar to other mints, it has more flavor intensity than the others.

Tasting Notes - NF
N: Wow, this might possibly be my favorite of all the smoked whiskeys! Upon initial nosing here is a big wave of fresh spearmint, crème de menthe, and very light smoke. It is much akin to smelling an ice-cold mint julep with a touch of smoke for interest.
P: Whereas the smoke was very gentle on the nose, it really comes through on the palate. The mint, while still present, takes more of a back seat to the campfire smoke.
F: In this short to mid-length finish, the spearmint does a curious thing by once again making a grand entrance.
C: This whiskey would make an excellent mint julep to sip on a hot summer day, but with the added element of smoke. One could even just add a cube of ice to it and make an instant mint julep, without needing to muddle real mint. I can imagine this smoked whiskey becoming a cult classic!

Tasting Notes - JN

N: Mint chocolate, just a hint of smoke, caramelized berries, some dried herbs like bay leaf, oregano and rosemary, hazelnut with skin.
P: Oops, there is far more smoke than expected, also a lot of pepper and freshness, dried herbs, again chocolate and the sweetness of ripe fruit.
F: Warm and refreshing at the same time, the mint remains lively and the chocolate turns into cocoa
C: A very good dinner whiskey! Just smell it instead of having an aperitif and enjoy it with the dessert, preferably something with milk chocolate. This is such a great match!

JUNIPER

Description
Juniper trees are evergreen trees native to Europe and Asia. Juniper has a rich tradition in folklore for warding off evil spirits. The berries are very fragrant and oily. In the world of alcoholic beverages, it is best known as the main flavor in gin.

Tasting Notes - NF
N: Another very surprising whiskey in that the nose does not smell much like the strong, piney fragrance of juniper. I was expecting an aroma much like that of a classic gin. However, there is a good amount of candy-like sweetness, or maybe even bread baked with honey and raisins.

P: It is on the palate that the juniper really shines through, with notes of pine, orange citrus, fresh herbs, ground black pepper, and sweet smoke.

F: The finish is short, but nice and sweet!

C: All in all, a good dram, although the juniper notes do not come through as intensely as one might expect.

Tasting Notes - JN

N: Lively juniper! This could be mistaken for a barrel aged gin! Brown spices, caramel, smoke in the distance.

P: The juniper is again dominant; it shows the same floral note as in other juniper spirits. But all the other aromas stand alone, the peppery spices and the smoke do not really combine with the juniper, therefore the whiskey seems to be a bit unbalanced.

F: Again! The floral site of the juniper stays for a while, but now it gives other aromas only a small chance to show up.

C: What really intrigued me on the nose disappointed my tongue. Not even the sip of tonic water which I added to my whiskey could turn it to the better.

TARRAGON

Description
Tarragon is a perennial, aromatic culinary herb important to many styles of cooking, especially French cuisine. It is the main flavoring component of bearnaise sauce. It is also used in soft drinks in Eastern European countries. Medicinally it has also been used as a cure for hiccups.

Tasting Notes - NF
N: Faint aromas of tarragon waft up through the glass, but curiously the tarragon is not as prominent as one might imagine. However, this is still an incredibly herbal whiskey, with a hint of thyme and oregano thrown in.

P: All the above herbal notes can be found on the palate, as well as some fresh hay, a hint of orange citrus, toffee, and browned butter. I'm surprised to even find some candied ginger as well!

F: Mid-length, with waves of herbs mid palate.

C: I enjoy the savory herbal aromas and flavors of this whiskey. It is a little more gentle than some, and does not have as much of the "meaty" quality of the other smoked whiskeys.

Tasting Notes - JN

N: Sweet spiced wine, layers of honey and overripe fruit, rum raisins, creamy milk chocolate, drying herbs, slightly floral.
P: Not as sweet as on the nose but there is still a winey note, lots of herbs and oriental scents, roasted nuts and seeds, but nearly no smoke.
F: Middle long, the spices and herbs get a smoky touch.
C: The very first moment I smelled this whiskey I got the feeling like being beamed into the heart of a medieval market. Here in Europe many old castles or even castle ruins offer such annual events with knight's tournaments, dungeon dinners, food and drink, while most attendees are wearing handmade perfectly copied armor and garment. Usually the chefs at this kind of events follow medieval recipes to prepare authentic food; and you might imagine what kind of luscious and opulent aromas hit the nose. You'll find everything in this whiskey – a real cracker!

VIOLET

Description
Violet is a genus of flowering plants of European origin. Violets have been used in folk medicine for millennia. It is cultivated for its beautiful and fragrant flowers.

Tasting Notes - NF
N: As the name suggests, the prominent aroma from this whiskey is smoked violets! The nose is intensely floral, both with violet and rose potpourri. Notes of shaved cedar can be found underneath the floral top notes. Upon second and third pass come some uncharacteristic notes of Twinkie® cream, oatmeal cake, and fried plantain.
P: Wow, the violet and rose potpourri that was so distinct on the nose completely dissipate into an astringent sea of smoked cedar and hickory.
F: The long finish is quite dry with a bitter, burning rubbish-like smoke. I find this finish to be somewhat unpleasant due to the bitter smoky dryness. The smoke envelops the palate, and has an oily, clinging quality about it.
C: This whiskey ranks up there among the most unusual of the smoked whiskeys I have tasted. Again, one would expect the more floral elements to dominate, but I found so many unique and interesting aromas that I was highly intrigued. It is not my favorite among the smoked whiskeys, but one cannot quarrel with its unusualness!

Tasting Notes - JN
N: A kind of "dirty" smoke, quite dusty, warm Christmas spices, overripe fruit, only a few floral spots in the distance.
P: The smoke is very obvious, still a kind of dirty, much dryer than expected, burned herbs.
F: Towards the end of the middle long finish there is again a floral note making its way through the smoke, but it doesn't help to soften the bitterness.
C: Can you imagine a purple violet, a fragile blossom with a fragrant smell? OK, then you know that this whiskey is the total opposite. It has more aromas of ironworks in the old times. This mixture of coal, steam and transmission oil-than of a plant which is admired for its finesse.

WORMWOOD

Description
Artemisia absinthium is a herbaceous perennial native to Africa and Eurasia. Wormwood has a long history in alcoholic beverage production and was used instead of hops as a bittering agent in beer and as a spice in mead in the Middle Ages. It is a primary ingredient in the spirit absinthe and is also used in bitters, vermouth, gin, and liqueurs. Wormwood has a reputation as a hallucinogen, which has been disproved by modern science.

Tasting Notes - NF
N: This is one of the most unusual whiskey aromas I have ever nosed. The wormwood, sage brush-like notes are very prominent to the exclusion of most everything else. This whiskey is more like smoked absinthe rather than smoked whiskey.
P: More sagebrush, white absinthe, bay leaf and desert dust.
F: Again, the pungent sagebrush notes completely dominate and create a very long, somewhat bitter finish.
C: This whiskey reminds me of the aromas of the high desert, with lots dustiness and dryness.

Tasting Notes - JN

N: Lively citrus aromas, coal smoke and warm glimmering fire, dried herbs and spices like turmeric,
P: Still a lot of citrus and the smoke is a bit stronger; the bitterness of the wormwood is dominating and leaves nearly no space for other aromas.
F: The bitterness is increasing and makes the whiskey very medicinal. If this were absinthe a few drops of water would help, but the haze is not too strong and the bitterness stays, so we can be sure that this is whiskey.
C: The taste washed some memory into my brain because it reminded me so much of the wormwood tea my Mum always forced me to drink when I had stomach problems in my early years. The tea was so bitter that I always had to hold my nose when gulping it down, otherwise it emptied my stomach immediately. You see, it did help, either for the good or the bad. But, to be honest, I don't need this kind of childhood memory anymore.

BLENDING

Design your whiskey to be great, don't just hope for greatness

I'm always amazed at how many new distillers I meet who have the mindset of throwing a bunch of different grains in a mash tun in the hopes of making an award winning whiskey. A high class dram is planned and designed. It doesn't just happen by accident. You have to actively visualize what you want, then make it a reality. Guess-work in the mash tun is almost guaranteed failure.

The problem is that many people approach whiskey making without a unique voice. They just want to make a standard bourbon or malt whiskey, often retreading the footsteps of so many distillers before them. Whiskey should be dynamic and should be imprinted with some personality. Make it personal and you can make it well. What have you never tried? What would be new for you? What has never been done in a whiskey? Why has it not been done?

Draw on personal experience. For instance, I had some amazing chicory coffee in New Orleans, so I began to wonder how a smoked chicory whiskey would taste. Think about what's around you. Right now, I'm looking out my window at cedar and magnolia trees. What would a smoked whiskey taste like if I smoked the malt with magnolia or cedar wood? I may do an experiment with those two tonight! I was raised in the South, so I lean towards many of the trees that are easy for me to get. When you open yourself up to using ingredients outside of the standard whiskey toolbox, the sheer breadth of possibilities can be as daunting as it is liberating.

Think you aren't creative or unique? You're wrong. There are 6 billion people on the planet. They all have unique fingerprints, unique DNA....and unique minds. Find out what is unique about you, what is around you. What was your favorite tree to climb as a kid? How about an herb you loved smelling from your childhood? Even if people do not like your whiskey, at least you made something unique. There are 450 bourbon brands right now. Does the world need another?

Flavor complexity

One of the keys to making a whiskey that will be judged well in competition is to pay attention to the three components you will be judged by: the nose, the palate, and the finish. The nose(N) is the initial aroma at the front of the whiskey BEFORE you drink. The palate(P), or body of the whiskey, is when you drink, but before you swallow. The palate includes the flavors tasted all around your tongue as well as the overall mouthfeel. The finish(F) is the tail end of the whiskey tasting AFTER you have swallowed. If any of these three are weak, your whiskey will be judged harshly. This is why blending different types of smoke flavors together is so important to making a whiskey that is exciting at every

phase for the drinker. Many smoke flavors are good on the nose or finish, but not the body and vice versa. Many smoked whiskeys fail because the distiller hasn't considered what will work best for all three parts of the dram's existance. I believe that Corsair has been successful with our smoked whiskeys, in part, because we blend extensively with so many different smokes and make sure that every whiskey hits all the right notes.

Nose – I strive for a pleasant smoke that is alluring and builds anticipation, but isn't too overpowering. Acrid or off aromas related to smoke will cloud the tasters opinion before they even drink it. Overall the nose should make the drinker WANT to taste the spirit. Fruit woods are great here because of their pleasant sweetness. Cherry is one of my favorites though pear, mulberry, and apple are all great as well. Herbs can create extra uniqueness, but can bleed acrid off-flavors into the finish of the whiskey.

Palate – Here I want a good solid smoke character and maybe some unique flavors thrown in for complexity. "Easter eggs," or subtle flavors that might not be immediately detectable, are good to put in here as the drinker is rewarded for coming back to the spirit again and again. Blending different types of smoke allows you to hit slightly different flavors at each of the three phases of the dram. If the shift is too jarring the drinker may not like it, but a subtle surprise is always good and keeps people fascinated with your spirit.

Finish – I like a nice long finish that leaves a lasting pleasant taste in the throat and the mind of the taster.

You may think the body, or palate, is the most important aspect of tasting a whiskey. However, I really believe the finish is what stays in the judge's mind the longest. The nose provides the first impression of the whiskey, and the flavor on the palate provides ample reason to mull over a whiskey's virtues, but the finish is the final and most lingering aspect of the dram. A long finish will stay in the mind of the taster well after the glass has been emptied. If you have a nice pleasant smoky finish, the judge will reward you with a positive mark. Most of our taste perception is based on smell; however alcohol is unique because even after you have drunk it, there is aftertaste in your mouth and throat and it is still evaporating, so that you taste it long after it is gone. Take advantage of this!

Changing space and time

When I use a stopwatch and time myself drinking a dram of fire water, it usually goes something like this: I hold it up to my nose and smell it for 1-2 seconds, drink the whiskey and hold it in my mouth for 3-4 seconds. I like to hold it in my mouth and really taste it, moving it over every part of my tongue and cheeks. (It helps to breath in a little through your mouth, passing air over the whiskey. This will bring out some of the more volatile aromatics.) I then swallow it, which takes another second. From the time I swallow to when the taste of the whiskey is gone from my mouth is the finish. That pleasant burn is what whiskey connoisseurs love and casual whiskey drinkers dislike. This usually lasts another 4-5 seconds. The finish length can be quite variable with bourbons often finishing faster than most single malts. It tends to be even longer with a smoky Scotch like an Islay. An oily spirit like gin or absinthe will linger even more on the tongue. I once believed the finish to be a difficult parameter to manipulate with regards to affecting a whiskey's overall character. It turns out I was wrong.

Certain types of smoke can really change the length of the finish of the whiskey. Oily smoke fuel sources like lemon wood, orange wood, and olive wood can really change the length of time of the finish. The oils also have an amazing ability to pick up other flavors and carry them through to the finish. Blending olive wood and cherry wood together extends the pleasant sweetness of the cherry through to the end of the finish in a way that cherry wood smoke by itself does not. The sweetness of cherry wood by itself peters out before the finish is completely over with. When blended with other smoke types it really changes the length of the finish. Some smokes will actually shorten the finish such as red oak.

The following table was generated from informal tastings and illustrates general finish lengths for various whiskeys.

SMOKE / SPIRIT	LENGTH OF FINISH TIME
Standard Bourbon	5 seconds
Apple	7 seconds
Olive	18 seconds
Orange	21 seconds
Lemon	35+ seconds

The nose is another parameter that we can change over time to the drinker. I want the drinker to be able to smell the whiskey the second they take the top off the bottle. My wife can typically smell me opening my blending kit in the next room, before I've even tried anything. This ability to build anticipation is very important. Typically this happens on the nose, when someone smells the spirit before they put it in their mouth. A stronger and aromatic nose will force the drinker to contemplate the whiskey before they even tip the glass back.

Mouthfeel is another important parameter that can be changed by the type of smoke. Oily fuel sources like the citrus trees tend to thicken the mouthfeel substantially and make the spirit feel larger in volume than it really is. Some grains used in the base whiskey can also change mouthfeel. One of my favorites is oats. Oats really seem to thicken up the body of a whiskey. When used in conjunction with smoked malt, it makes the spirit taste "meatier."

Begin with the end in mind

I once saw an interview with the film director James Cameron. He said that he puts the most effort into the last 20 minutes of a film, as that is what the audience remembers. Many failed film directors have movies that are very exciting in the beginning yet run out of steam towards the end, leaving the filmgoers disappointed. I believe the same can be said for whiskey.

I meet a lot of aspiring distillers who ask me the secret to making good whiskey. Aromatics, flavor, and finish are all important, and you should strive for interest in all three. If you can make all three slightly different, you create a pleasant diversity and flavor complexity that will make people come back to your whiskey again and again. However, if you botch the ending you will pay dearly for it. With smoked whiskeys, acrid 'burning rubber' tastes and sulfury aromas are often the worst offenders. These flavors can develop with almost any fuel source, but certain hardwoods and a few herbs seem to be the biggest culprits. Luckily there are some great finishing fuel types that can really change and save the end of many smoke blend whiskeys. For instance, maple creates one of the most fascinating finishes, leaving a sweet and intriguing twist to the whiskey. If you can end with a dynamic finish, people will continue to come back to your whiskey.

Easter Eggs

I also like to occasionally throw in a tiny amount of a very signature smoke. Sage is a great example. Even at a tiny percentage, say 1%, you can faintly pick up on it if you try. Hardcore whiskey geeks and judges are proud of the time they have put into developing their palates and noses. If you put in subtle Easter eggs for them to find, you will build a rabid following amongst the most hardcore whiskey lovers. This is another great aspect of smoked whiskeys: the ability to have layers and layers of complexity. Like an onion being peeled back to reveal new layers, the more you drink it the more Easter eggs you find. I want someone to come back to my whiskey and find new aromas and flavors every time.

Blending can sometimes be a dirty word in whiskey making because "blends" are considered (strangely) less interesting types of whiskey than single malts. But when making smoked whiskeys with something other than peat, you will often find yourself lacking if you only use one smoke type. There are a very few smoke types that can create complex whiskeys by themselves. For the most part, it's best to mix different whiskeys that are strong in the nose, palate, or finish to make for a whiskey with more depth and nuance. The goal is to make sure there is a fairly even smoke level throughout the complete experience for the whiskey drinker.

Building flavors

Different types of fuel sources each have their own character. In general the hardwoods create the best neutral smoke character and the pleasant "distant campfire" aroma that many people connect to a memory of their childhood. The fruit woods have a wonderful sweetness that is comforting to even the most ardent smoke-hater. The citrus woods are like nothing else. Their intense flavors completely change the mouthfeel of the whiskey due to the oils and citrusy flavors they produce. They are very distinctive, but can overpower a blend quickly. Maple wood creates the most unique finish of any fuel source. Any of the wood smoke flavors below except the lemon can stand on their own with no blending. It is no secret that Corsair is in love with cherry smoked malts and we have experimented extensively with cherry wood. It is the dominant smoke character in our award winning Triple Smoke whiskey.

The following are my personal favorites of the different types of fuel sources, with the top one in the list being my favorite of the group:

Wood
maple wood
avocado
lemon
mulberry
pear
cherry

The herbs have more character and more signature aromas. However they can rarely be used by themselves, as they often get a bitter and acrid finish. They are unique and can add a lot of flavor complexity.

Herbs
lemon balm
sage
skullcap

The barks and roots are more smokey than the herbs, but still almost as unique and full of character. They don't have the firepower smoke-wise of the hardwoods. The flavors tend to be very interesting, but weak on the nose and like the herbs, can often develop an acrid finish. A few of these, like cascara, are so strong as to be able to be used by themselves and carry the entire spirit's nose, body, and finish with exceptional character and uniqueness while maintaining balance.

Barks/Root
cascara bark
blackberry root
fringe tree bark
muira puama bark
quassia bark

Barrel Woods
The barrel woods are interesting for their ability to retain the character of their previous contents. The cabernet wine barrel is a good example of this. When burned you can smell wine in the air mixed with smoke. When used in a whiskey the character of the wine comes through but in a subtle pleasant way and more on the nose than the finish.

Barrels
Cabernet Barrel Wood
French Oak Barrel Wood

Flavor types and compatibility
An example recipe
Here is an example blend to illustrate the concept. This blend will use three of my favorites.

40 % Pear – adds a pleasant and alluring sweet smoke to the nose
30% White Oak – Solid base smoke
30% Maple – adds a unique finish

White oak wood is just a great base wood. It has a strong, punchy smoke, but no finish, and it is not very distinctive. Pear wood is a fruit wood that is mild like all fruit woods, and has a great sweetness on the nose. The smoke character is very distinctive and is more pronounced than the oak. Sadly it tends to lose something on the finish. The finish is still pleasant and sweet, but it is not strong enough to stand on its own. Maple is the opposite, with a nice long finish, but almost zero nose. It adds a wonderful long smokiness that ends with a sweet and distinctive maple finish. These three different types of smoke blended together result in a dramatically more complex whiskey that changes over time, for the better.

Blend favorites
The collection below includes blends we have been playing around with for a while, and I believe they showcase some of the best and most complementary flavor associations.

Firehawk
Muira Puama   44%
White Oak   24%
Maple   32%

This is a variation on the blend above.
Notes: I am really proud of this blend. Andrew Webber (Corsair's cofounder) and I spent a lot of time on this blend and we both really felt it captured the best of what we had learned from these experiments. In this blend the white oak builds a strong base smoke character. White oak is just a great all around smoke flavor. The muira puama is a fascinating smoke that adds complexity to the nose, but it is too weak to exist by itself. The

maple is our secret weapon. It adds an amazing twist at the end that serves as a pleasant surprise to the drinker. A wonderfully smokey ending turns to a maple syrup over pancakes flavor. The drinker may have to try the spirit several times to lock in on the flavor, but will no doubt create an emotional connection to the spirit as it will take them back to having waffles or pancakes at grandma's house. At least that is what it does for me. If you can create these kind of intense associations, you'll build fans for life. The more I try this blend, the more flavors I keep finding in it.

Naga
Barberry   80%
Clove   20%

Notes: This is a spicy and intense blend not for the casual

whiskey drinker, however it is incredibly rewarding if you are looking for a unique experience. It may remind the drinker of a spiced rum, due to the very signature clove smell. The barberry just seems to work with the clove in a way that few other smokes could. This is an incredibly unique blend that shows the versatility of smoke flavors. It's not for everyone, and that's a good thing.

Meraxes
Rye whiskey base
Olive   15%
Guava   60%
Ash   25%

Notes: The rye whiskey base is the best vehicle to let these three stand out. Here the ash wood acts as a general smoke base and does the heavy lifting in the body of the smoke profile. The olive is a unique wood that is unlike other fruit or nut woods and more like a citrus wood. It adds a burning and oily element that changes the mouthfeel and creates an unusually long gin like finish. It also adds an herbal aroma to the nose. One would never know that olive wood is the culprit. So what about the guava? Guava is very pleasant and keeps this blend balanced. It adds tropical fruit elements to the nose and ends on a very pleasant smoke finish, which also helps balance the oily olive aftertaste.

Vermithrax
Amaranth whiskey base
Almond   10%
Pecan   40%
Mullein   50%

Notes: Pecan is similar to hickory and is a great smoke base. The almond, though a nut wood, it adds more fruit and lily smoke to the nose. The mullein adds a eucalyptus flavor and a very unusual oily and herbal element to the body and finish. Amaranth whiskey is unusual in its ability as a spirit base to amplify the pleasant 'distant campfire' smell that make many of these whiskeys so pleasant. I have no idea why the amaranth does this, but it really adds an amazing pop to the whiskey.

Black Cat
Quinoa whiskey base
Butternut Bark 25%
Avocado   70%
Mugwort   5%

Notes: Avocado adds a sweet nose with mild citrus notes to the nose and finish. The butternut bark causes the finish to end on the wonderful "distant campfire" smell while also sweetening the nose. The bitter mugwort is there to balance out the sweetness, but be careful; a little mugwort goes a long way. The quinoa adds an earthiness and changes the mouthfeel which pairs nicely with the honey notes of the avocado.

Vhagar
Nectarine	75%
Sage	25%

Notes: Sage is by far one of the most intense and uniquely signature smoke flavors I have come across. The nectarine is a pleasant sweet smoke that can help balance the intensity of the sage.

Rhaegal
Cabernet Barrel	40%
Black Walnut	45%
Manuka Wood	15%

Notes: The black walnut quickly became a staff favorite at Corsair. It is a solid and pleasant smoke that is strong during N,P, and F. The manuka beefs up the body. The star of this blend is the cabernet barrel smoked finish where a very distinct wine like character comes out.

Viserion
White Willow Bark	60%
Blackberry Root	25%
Lilac	15%

Notes: White willow bark has been one of my favorites since I first began experimenting with barks. The blackberry root is a pleasant and good all-around smoke. These two just seemed to work well together. The lilac actually adds some herbal elements even though no herbs were smoked. The lilac is another good wood that adds pleasant character to all stages of the dram.

Valryon
Sage	20%
Fringe Tree	50%
Cherry	30%

Notes: Once again here is a sage blend. This time it is paired with cherry wood to add some sweetness and to balance the intense sage aroma. Fringe tree is a solid favorite of mine and very pleasant to keep the sage from taking the blend in a harsh direction.

Silverwing
Lemon Balm	60%
Hickory	30%
Blackberry	10%

Notes: Lemon balm stood out as the clear winner of the herbal smoke flavor profiles. It just created an incredibly pleasant floral smoke with a huge range of aromas. The lemon balm can easily stand on its own in all three of the different parts of the drink: nose, body, and finish. The hickory beefs up the base, while the blackberry adds a soothing finish.

Ghiscar
Grape Vine   40%
Mulberry Wood   25%
Black Walnut   15%
Coffee   20%

Notes: The coffee wood is one of my favorites for its versatility in adding punch to the nose and finish of a whiskey. Coffee wood can easily stand on its own with no other woods. However, the black walnut is such a strong "backbone" smoke that strengthens and showcases the other smokes in this blend. Mulberry helps soften the nose while the grape adds an oiliness that changes the mouthfeel of the finish and makes the coffee aroma stick to the back of the drinker's throat. All of the oily smokes dramatically lengthen the finish of the whiskey. When attached to a strong flavor such as the coffee, it forces the drinker to contemplate this aroma for a long time after the drink has ended.

Essovius
Avocado   60%
Quassia   20%
Ash Wood   10%
Cabernet Barrel Wood   10%

Notes: The avocado adds some great sweet and orange-like aromas to the nose and contributes to a long finish. The cabernet adds jammy notes and a great sweet twist to the finish, as warm red wine notes round out at the very end. The quassia bark adds some dark fruit notes and the ash wood adds to the finish.

Archonel
Peach Wood   40%
Black Walnut   25%
Maple   15%

Notes: The peach wood adds a wonderful fruity sweetness, but in a way different from apple, pear, and cherry. Black walnut is just a great go-to base smoke. The maple adds its wonderful sweet finish, but in a subtle and balanced fashion.

Balerion
Olive   27%
White Oak   70%
Lemon   3%

Notes: The white oak is just a good, solid bed of smoke

flavor to build the rest of this blend around. It is especially strong on the palate, but is a bit weak on the nose. The olive wood smoke adds some briney characteristics similar to a Scotch, yet also adds some strong herbal character to the nose. The lemon, even at a tiny percentage, adds an intensity to the entire blend that is unforgettable and has a very long and citrusy finish.

Complicated smoke profiles:

Hydra
Apple	10%
Pear	30%
Black Walnut	20%
White Oak	15%
Cascara	25%

Notes: The fruit woods of apple and pear start this blend off with some sweetness and a pleasant nose. The white oak and black walnut do the heavy lifting in the middle of the spirit while the cascara adds some uniqueness without being overpowering. Any one of these could stand on their own; this blend is sort of an all-stars list from our experiments.

Tiamat
Hickory	25%
Avacodo	25%
Black Walnut	30%
Mulberry	16%
Orange	3%
Lemon	1%

Notes: This is an incredibly complex smoked whiskey that you can go back to again and again and keep discovering new flavors. The dangerous thing here is the orange and lemon combo. These citrus woods can really blow out the spirit and take over, but used in lesser amounts they really fill out the spirit. Mulberry and black walnut both have a wonderful character.

Combustion Hellfire
This blend was just plain nuts. We took every possible type of smoked whiskey and mixed it together. At least 50 different whiskeys were used. By about 25 different types of smoke, it was a very interesting and obviously complex whiskey. However as we kept adding more and more it began losing certain interesting characteristics. Acrid and harsh smoke flavors seemed to compound. Finally it resulted in a nasty whiskey that was totally unbalanced and a disappointment. I did include this anecdote here to show the danger of how off flavors can build up.

Summary
Blending different types of smoke together is a way to make a whiskey with more complexity and interest. By making sure the nose, palate, and finish are all strong, you will make a more balanced whiskey that will score better in competitions. The finish is the most important, as it is what drinkers remember the most. Woods tend to have better smoke flavor, but are not as distinctive. Herbs and barks are usually more unique, but have a better chance of developing acrid off-flavors.

SMOKY COCKTAILS
BY CHARLES CHRISTIAN FIELDS

RAFFLES JULEP
1.5 OZ SMOKED WHISKEY
2 OZ FRESH SOUR
.5 OZ SODA
.25 OZ LEMONGRASS SYRUP
FRESH MINT
SHAKE, STRAIN
SERVE IN HIGHBALL OVER ICE
GARNISH WITH FRESH MINT

SEAHAWK
2 OZ SMOKED WHISKEY
4 OZ GINGER BEER
JUICE FROM ONE LIME
GARNISH WITH SALTED CUCUMBER
STIR INGREDIENTS IN A PILSNER GLASS

FLINT LOCK
1.5 OZ SMOKED WHISKEY
.5 OZ ROSE WATER
.5 OZ MINERAL WATER
GARNISH WITH FIG PRESERVE
STIR, STRAIN
SERVE ON ROCKS
WITH A SPOON OF FIG PRESERVE

CAPTAINS CAP
1.5 OZ SMOKED WHISKEY
1/2 MUDDLED ORANGE
1 OZ STOUT BEER
SHAKE, STRAIN WELL, TOP WITH STOUT
GARNISH WITH BURNT ORANGE PEEL

APPLESEED
2 OZ SMOKED WHISKEY
4 OZ SPARKLING CIDER
2 THIN SLICES OF FRESH GINGER
SERVE ON ROCKS IN PILSNER GLASS, GARNISH WITH GINGER
AND A DASH OF ANGOSTURA BITTERS

SANTA GOLD

1.5 OZ SMOKED WHISKEY
1 OZ HEAVY CREAM
2 TSP RAW SUGAR
2 TSP CLOVER HONEY
EGG WHITE
1 DASH VANILLA EXTRACT
SHAKE VIGOROUSLY TO EMULSIFY EGG WHITE, STRAIN, GARNISH WITH FEE BROTHERS AZTEC CHOCOLATE BITTERS

KINGSTON CUP
1.5 OZ SMOKED WHISKEY
1 TBS RAW SUGAR
FRESH PINEAPPLE
MUDDLE PINEAPPLE AND SUGAR
ADD WHISKEY, SHAKE, STRAIN
SERVE OVER ICE,
TOP WITH GINGER ALE
SERVE IN HIGHBALL
GARNISH WITH PINEAPPLE CUBE

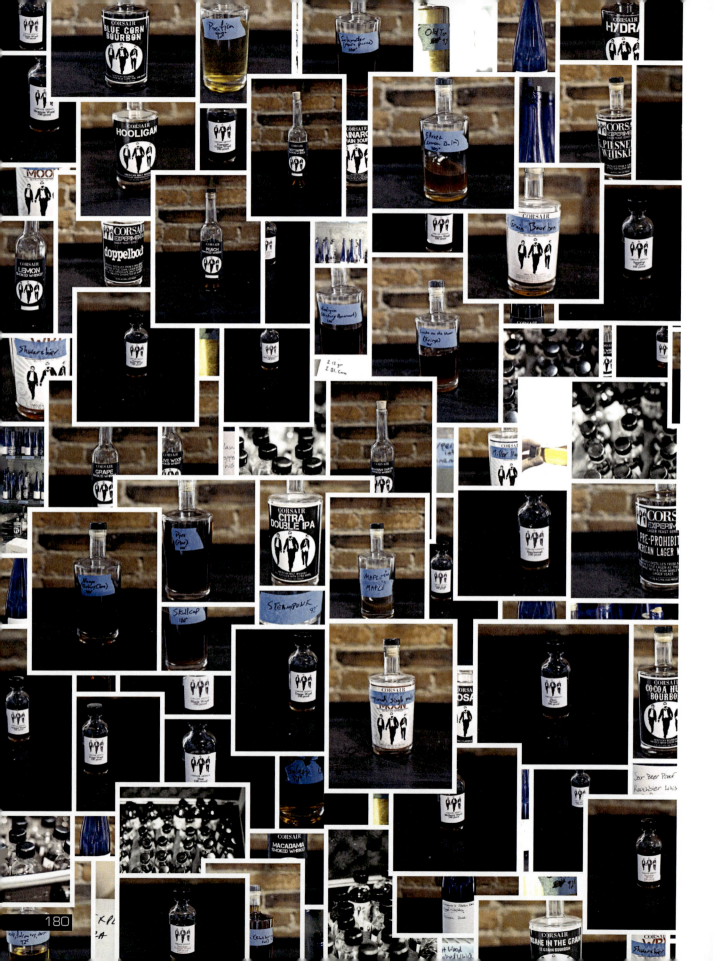

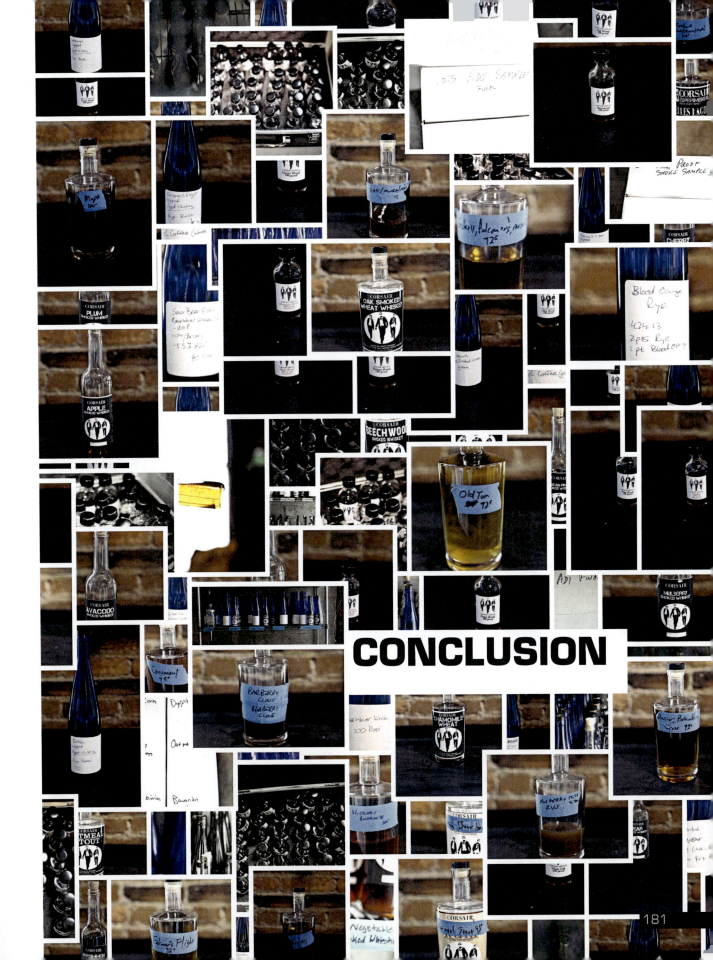

CONCLUSION

So what is the best?

If there is one question people have asked me the most it is this one. It is really, really hard for me to answer. People want a simple answer like "use hickory smoke and you will win a million awards and be a darling in all the drinks magazines." Sadly, the answer is a lot more complicated. I like many of these, which is why I hired two third party noses in Julia Nourney and Nancy Fraley. I won't speak for them but simply tell you my favs. You love all your children and it is hard to choose only one. I also become more attached to some woods that took a lot more work, and therefore I became more invested in. Lemon wood was a total pain to smoke and deal with. I spent a lot more time on it, and feel more proud of this work, and therefore more biased. The main complication is that many fuel types are amazing on the nose, but not the finish, or vice versa. Ideally, you need to blend them for maximum effect. All right, time to face the music.

My favorites

In general I love the fruit woods, because they have an amazing nose. However, they need to be blended with something else. Fruit woods have a wonderful sweetness. Of these, we have won a number of awards with our cherry wood smoked bourbon, including "American Whiskey of the Year" from the Wizards of Whisky awards. However, another fruit wood barely beats it: pear. Mulberry also comes in right after pear.

Pear - Pear wood is similar to apple wood and cherry wood but barely edges them out as it is more distinct than apple yet cleaner than both on the finish. Even at very high proof without being proofed down with water there is no sulfury or petroleum like off flavors that are the bane of many of our experiments. Hands down, pear wood was the top fruit wood.

Maple - Maple has an incredible finish that makes for a truly unique whiskey experience. It is just fascinating, yet comforting, as it makes you think of having pancakes as a kid. It is weak on the nose and must be blended.

Black Walnut - This smoke was the top of the nut woods, by far. It was a solid smoke that had character in the nose, body, and finish yet remained clean with the pleasant "distant campfire" flavor we all came to enjoy.

White Oak - For a big meaty smoke, white oak is a great foundation smoke, easily beating hickory smoke, mesquite, and alder.

Lemon Wood - Of the citrus woods, the lemon was just so over the top and intense. It also has the ability to extend the finish over time and carry other flavors through the finish, similar to gin.

Lemon Balm - In the category of herbs, lemon balm beats out sage due to its overall pleasantness, distinctiveness, and strong scoring across the nose, body, and finish. Solid all around.

Cacara Bark - This smoke flavor was incredibly unique and intense while remaining smooth.

Cabernet Barrel Wood - Of the barrel woods, this one really brought across the wine and grape aromas of the product that had sat in the barrel, adding wonderful flavor complexity and a truly unique whiskey experience yet still had a very clean smoke taste.

What did my judges think? This is from Julia Nourney:

Final thoughts

After finishing the sampling I had a look at the tasting notes of my colleague and friend Nancy, just to find out if we both have similar feelings about these whiskeys. And while I was comparing our notes I realized that we mostly have the same basic thoughts about sweet, sour, bitter, etc. but we both made totally different experiences while we grew up and developed our sensory. It was not just that our mothers fed us different things; it is the whole eating culture that divides both sides of the pond.

It made me smile to read how many different barbecue and tomato sauces or sandwich spreads Nancy knows and how she described it. We don't have such products in our shops and the few American brands we can buy here are mostly available in specialist shops. Nancy also mentioned so many different dishes which I have never heard of but I am quite sure that you, dear reader, are familiar with. And on the other hand I am quite sure that there are many dishes and flavours I have mentioned that you are not aware of. And additionally it might also be a language problem because I am not a mother tongue speaker (which – I am sure – you have already found out) which probably makes it extra difficult for you to follow my impressions.

I sometimes work as a judge for spirits competitions and it is always interesting to have Americans in the panel because they judge spirits completely different than judges from Europe or Asia do. Americans are very well known (and also feared) for judging obvious aromas quite high while judges from other parts of the world prefer mostly subtle and sometimes even hiding aromas. That might make it easier to understand why some products are successful differently here and there.

This is also the reason why I think that these whiskeys satisfy the American taste better than the European one because some of the flavours are so striking that they tax European tongues. On the other hand I am sure that most aromas in these whiskeys open up a new dimension to people who have never had such an experience... and this is probably one of the most enjoyable things in life! Don't miss it!

This was a tough decision. My "top twelve" are:
- Beechwood
- Cabernet Barrel Wood
- Grape Wood
- Lemon Wood
- Manzanita Wood
- Maple Wood
- Orange Wood
- Peach Wood
- Peat
- Pecan Wood
- Plum Wood

I had the hard job to turn down a few more, which I also liked very much. On 13th to 15th place are:

Birch Wood, Jamaican Pimento Wood, and Mesquite Wood.

Best

Julia
Julia Nourney
Independent Spirits Consultant
Whisk(e)y, Cognac, Grappa, fruit spirits, Calvados

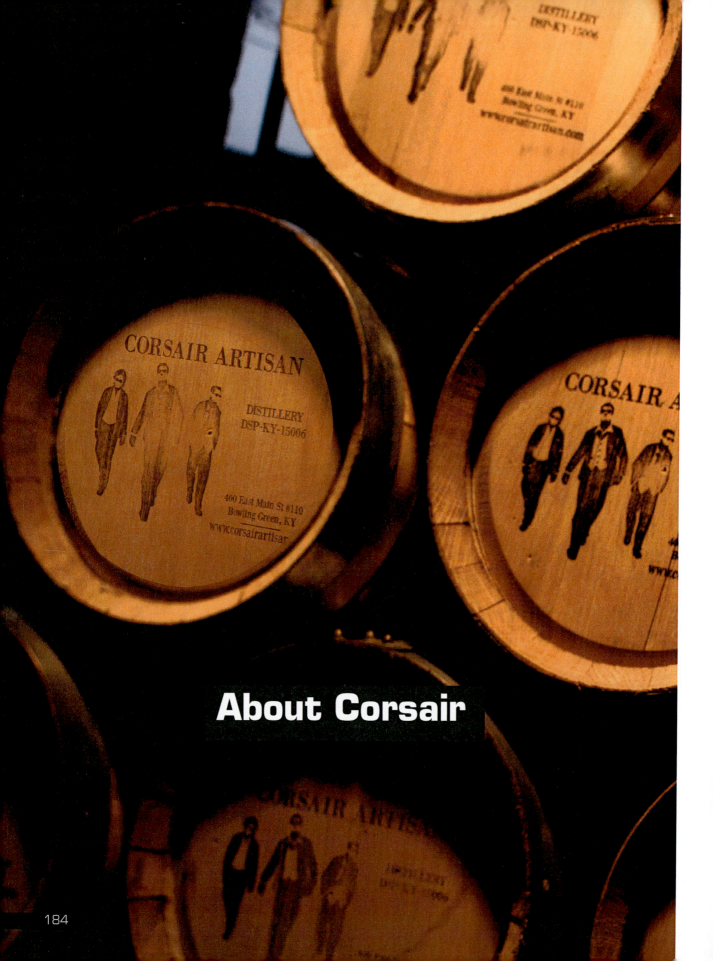

About Corsair

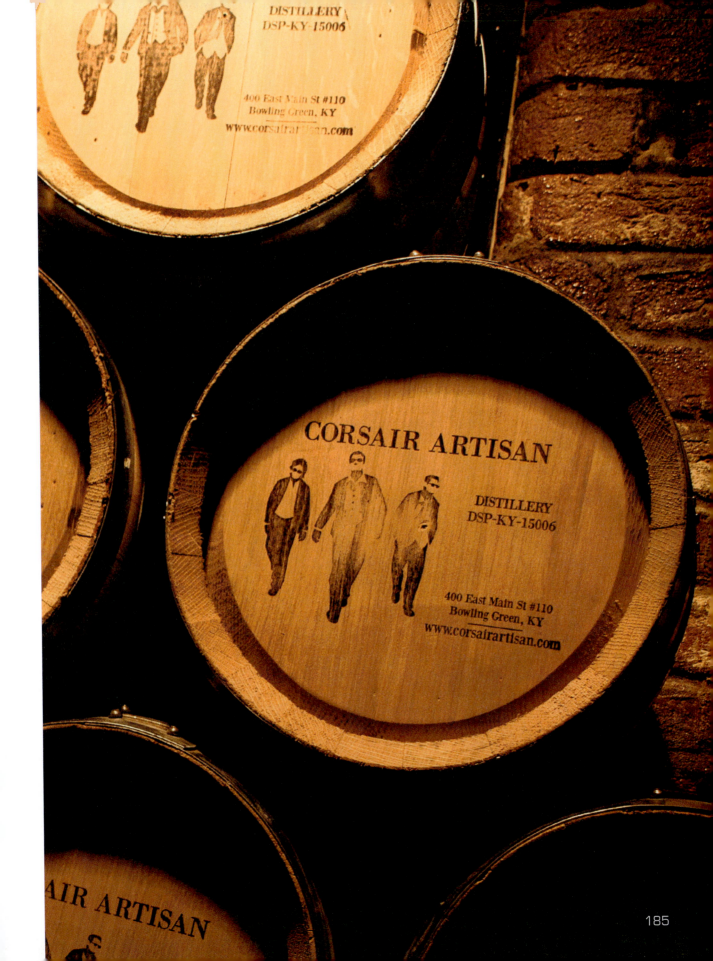

Story

Childhood friends Darek Bell and Andrew Webber began home brewing beer and wine in Darek and Amy Lee Bell's garage. They hit a snag while working on a prototype biodiesel plant, causing Andrew to remark that making whiskey would be much more satisfying. The idea stuck, and the two soon found themselves studying distilleries and spirits. Soon after, Corsair Distillery was founded. Corsair's spirits have been praised in publications such as Food and Wine, Saveur, Imbibe, Whisky Magazine, Whisky Advocate, the Atlantic, Time Out New York, and Maxim.com. Corsair's innovative and adventurous spirits have won 67 medals at international spirits competitions. Whisky Magazine named Corsair the 2013 "Craft Distillery of the year" and "Brand Innovator of the Year." Whisky Advocate named Corsair's Triple Smoke Whiskey the 2013 "Artisan Whiskey of the Year." "Craft Distillery of the Year" for Wizards of Whisky and the American Distilling Institute's Bubble Cap award for Distillery of the Year.

AWARDS

2013 "Craft Distillery of the year." Whisky Magazine ICONS of Whisky Awards
2013 "Brand Innovator of the year." Whisky Magazine ICONS of Whisky Awards
2014 "Craft Distillery of the year." Wizards of Whisky
2014 "Craft Distillery of the year." American Distilling Institute Bubble Cap award.
2014 "Brand Innovator of the year" Whisky Magazine ICONS of Whisky Awards

AWARDS - SPIRITS

Triple Smoke
Artisan Whiskey of the Year, Whisky Advocate
Gold, 2010 San Francisco World Spirits Competition
Silver, 2010 American Distillers Institute Awards
Gold, 2010 International Review of Spirits Awards, BTI
Bronze, 2011 American Distillers Institute Awards
Gold, 2011 MicroLiquor Spirits Awards

Wry Moon
Double Gold, 2010 San Francisco World Spirits Competition
Silver, 2010 American Distillers Institute Awards
Pumpkin Spice Moonshine
Bronze, 2011 San Francisco World Spirits Competition
Bronze, 2011 MicroLiquor Spirits Awards

100% RYE
Silver, 2010 International Review of Spirits Awards, BTI
Bronze, 2010 American Distillers Institute Awards
Silver, 2011 American Distillers Institute Awards
Gold, 2011 MicroLiquor Spirits Awards

Ryemageddon
Silver, 2012 American Distillers Institute Awards
Rasputin Hopped Whiskey
Platinum, Best of Class, 2009 World Beverage Competition
Bronze, 2010 American Distillers Institute Awards
Bronze, 2011 American Distillers Institute Awards
Wormwood Wit Barrel Strength
Gold, 2010 American Distillers Institute Awards

Quinoa Whiskey
Silver, 2011 New York International Spirits Competition
Bronze, 2012 American Distillers Institute Awards

Barrel Aged Gin
Gold, 2011 San Francisco World Spirits Competition
Silver, 2012 NY International Spirits Competition

Gin
Gold, 2009 San Francisco World Spirits Competition
Gold, 2009 World Beverage Competition
Silver, 2011 MicroLiquor Spirits Awards
Gold, 2011 International Review of Spirits Awards, BTI

Graniac 9 Grain Bourbon
Best of Class, Best of Category, and Gold, 2012 American Distillers Institute Awards

Nashville Bourbon (Cherry Smoked Bourbon)
Silver, 2012 American Distillers Institute Awards

Czech Pils American Malt Whiskey
Silver, 2012 American Distillers Institute Awards

Oatmeal Stout Whiskey
Silver, 2012 American Distillers Institute Awards
Bronze, 2011 American Distillers Institute Awards

PreProhibition American Malt Whiskey
Silver, 2012 American Distillers Institute Awards

Oak Smoked Wheat Whiskey
Silver, 2012 American Distillers Institute Awards

Cherrywood Smoke
Bronze, 2012 American Distillers Institute Awards

Citra Whiskey
Best of Category, Gold, 2012 American Distillers Institute Awards

Elderflower Bohemian Whiskey
Bronze, 2012 American Distillers Institute Awards

Triticale Whiskey
Bronze, 2012 American Distillers Institute Awards

Hopmonster
Silver, NY International Spirits Competition Awards

Rasputin
Platinum, World Beverage Competition
Bronze, NY International Spirits Competition Awards

INDEX

A

absinthe, 36, 129, 155, 160
acetate, 66
acrospire, 32
alamosa, 79
alder, 12, 21, 66-67, 73, 184
allspice, 22, 84, 86, 98, 102, 108, 121, 129, 132
almond, 12, 21, 67, 69, 72, 94, 100, 103-104, 116, 142, 165
altwhiskeys, 198-199
amaranth, 18, 53, 165
amaretto, 67
amylase, 32
antibacterial, 118
antibiotic, 113
aperitif, 90, 136, 149
aphrodisiac, 118, 125, 135
apple, 12, 19, 21, 33, 66-70, 73, 76, 80, 82, 89, 91-92, 95, 100, 109, 136, 142, 159-160, 169-170, 184
apricot, 12, 21, 69, 75
ardbeg, 59

B

bamberger, 54
barberries, 66, 164-165
bark, 11, 13, 21-22, 38, 62, 73, 79, 89, 91, 97, 103, 105, 112-114, 116-125, 163, 165, 168-169, 171, 184, 199
barley, 8, 14, 20, 31, 33, 36, 45, 49-53, 59-60, 62, 97, 110
barrel, 8, 11-12, 19-21, 23, 35-36, 45-47, 52, 62, 76, 79, 90, 92, 106-111, 124, 150, 163, 168-169, 184-185, 189
basil, 145
bayberry, 13, 22, 113
beech, 12, 72-73, 114
beechnuts, 68
beechwood, 19, 21, 27, 45, 54, 72, 185
birch, 12-13, 21-22, 73-74, 114, 185
blueberry, 115, 128

i

189

botanicals, 20, 36, 47
bourbon, 12, 14-15, 18-19, 23, 51-52, 91, 108-109, 120, 158, 160, 184, 189
bowmore, 59
bruichladdich, 6, 8, 19, 59
buchi, 20
buckthorn, 117
buckwheat, 51-53, 57
bunnahabhain, 59
butternut, 13, 22, 116, 165
butterscotch, 72

C

cabernet, 12, 23, 109, 163, 168-169, 184-185
cacara, 184
calamus, 13, 22, 130
calvados, 185
campfire, 20, 39, 59, 66, 75, 78-79, 85-86, 95-96, 100-101, 116, 120, 130, 143, 145, 149, 162, 165, 184
carcinogen, 105
cardamom, 132
caribbean, 86, 121
carrots, 128-129
cascara, 13, 22, 117, 130, 163, 170
cashews, 69
catnip, 13, 22, 131
catuaba, 13, 22, 118
cedar, 12, 21, 66, 76-77, 84, 89, 97, 134, 152, 158
cherries, 12, 19-21, 54, 77, 83, 89, 91-92, 96-97, 99, 109-110, 119, 128, 135-136, 142, 159-160, 162-163, 168-169, 184, 189
cherrywood, 189
chutney, 68
cicely, 22
cider, 179
cilantro, 129
citra, 189
citrus, 21, 71, 79-80, 85, 87, 91, 95-96, 98-99, 101, 104, 113, 118-119, 122, 129, 134, 136, 143, 150-151, 155, 161-162, 165, 170, 184
clove, 13, 22, 38, 86, 132, 164-165

clover, 180
cocoa, 52, 70, 76, 83, 87, 89, 103-104, 106, 125, 128, 149
coconut, 82, 104, 111
coffee, 12, 23, 44-45, 52, 78, 101, 158, 169
coffey, 27
cognac, 92, 107, 185
colorado, 23, 51-52, 54, 57, 79
coniferous, 76, 114
coppa, 75, 117, 138
copper, 46
cordials, 94
coriander, 138
cotton, 37-38, 119
cottonwood, 12, 54, 57, 79
crabapple, 12, 21, 80
cranberry, 77, 88
creosote, 20, 44, 46
cucumber, 176
currant, 104, 109, 113-114, 123
curry, 111, 138, 144
cuts, 32, 45, 47

D

dill, 128-129
drupe, 101

E

eggplant, 52
eggs, 133, 159, 161-162
elderflower, 189
emmer, 52
endosperm, 32
enzymatic, 26
enzyme, 20, 26, 28, 32, 51-52, 54
eucalyptus, 94, 143, 165
evergreen, 76, 87, 98, 125, 150
extracts, 54

ii

F

faint, 75, 109, 132, 151
feijoada, 93
fennel, 78, 128-129, 144
fermentation, 19, 45-46, 62
feseenjoon, 77
fever, 113
fig, 72-73, 91, 114, 123, 134, 177
firehawk, 164
firewood, 70, 72-73
flambéed, 78, 103
fraxinus, 70
fruit, 21, 66-69, 71-72, 76-83, 86-89, 93-104, 108, 110, 117-119, 121-123, 128-129, 131, 134-136, 139, 144, 149, 151-152, 159, 162, 164-165, 169-170, 184-185

G

ghee, 67
gin, 18, 20-21, 36, 47, 87, 97, 107, 114, 129, 150, 155, 160, 165, 184, 189
ginger, 13, 22, 78, 88, 102, 105, 130, 133, 151, 176, 179, 181
gooseberry, 113
gouda, 90, 100
grain, 8, 20, 27-29, 31-33, 35, 37, 40, 44-47, 49-55, 59, 62, 79, 107-108, 114, 118-119, 189
grainarchy, 52
grainiac, 52
grape, 12, 21, 23, 81, 124, 169, 184-185
grapefruit, 80, 116, 143
grapevines, 81
grätzer, 54

H

habanera, 122
hazelnut, 70, 83-84, 103, 116, 149
hebridean, 27

herb, 11, 13, 21-22, 36, 38, 62, 86, 91, 112-114, 118, 120, 127, 129, 131-132, 136, 138-139, 142-146, 148-152, 155, 158-159, 161, 163, 168, 171, 184, 199
herbaceous, 131, 145, 148-149, 155
hickory, 12, 19, 21, 23, 33, 44, 57, 67, 85, 100-101, 152, 165, 168-170, 184
honey, 52, 66, 70-71, 90, 92-93, 95-96, 101, 110-111, 117, 120, 125, 142, 150-151, 165, 180
honeydew, 69
hopmonster, 189

I

iodine, 54, 81, 120, 130

J

jamaican, 12-13, 21-22, 84, 86, 98, 104, 120-121, 185
jammy, 169
jasmine, 13, 22, 121, 134-135
jerk, 86, 121
juniper, 13, 36, 68, 78, 94, 97, 102, 114, 150
juniperus, 76-77
jura, 27

K

kiawe, 12, 21, 83
kiln, 19, 26-29, 32-33, 35, 54, 59-60
kumquat, 116

L

lactic, 138
lagavulin, 44, 59
lamiaceae, 139, 148

iii

laphroaig, 59
lautering, 45-46
lavender, 13, 22, 134-135
leather, 69, 80, 84, 89, 92, 103, 117, 122-123
lemon, 12-13, 21-23, 63, 87, 97, 136, 160, 162-163, 168-170, 174, 184-185
lemongrass, 175
leptospermum, 90
lichtenhainer, 54
lilac, 12, 21, 70, 88, 168
lily, 67, 165
liquorice, 78, 105, 144

M

macadamia, 12, 21, 89
magnolia, 119, 158
malt, 4, 6, 8, 11, 18-20, 22-23, 25-33, 35-37, 44-46, 49, 51-57, 59-62, 66, 72, 75, 77, 79, 87, 91, 94, 98, 107, 110, 120, 123, 125, 144, 158, 160-162, 189
maltster, 27, 35, 46, 55-57, 79
maluku, 132
mango, 68, 78, 90, 108, 117, 119, 121, 128
manuka, 12, 45, 90, 95, 168
manzanita, 12, 21, 91, 185
maple, 12, 54-55, 92, 106, 116, 131, 161-164, 169, 184-185
maplewood, 21, 92
medicinal, 73, 86, 97, 113, 115-117, 119-120, 122, 124-125, 129-130, 138, 142, 146, 151, 155
menthe, 149
menthol, 94
mezcal, 66

N

nashville, 15, 77, 189
nectar, 90
nectarine, 12, 21, 96, 103, 168
nut, 21, 69, 71-72, 75, 78, 84, 87, 89, 92, 94, 100-101, 103, 106, 128, 151, 165, 170, 184

nutmeg, 84, 86-87, 101-103, 111, 121, 130

O

oat, 50, 52-53, 110, 161
oatmeal, 50, 110, 152, 189
ohia, 12, 21, 84
olea, 97
olive, 12, 70, 88, 97, 160, 165, 169-170
olivewood, 21
orange, 12, 21, 71, 78, 91, 93, 96, 98-99, 104, 114, 118-120, 132, 136, 138, 143, 150-151, 160, 169-170, 178, 185

P

papaya, 121
paprika, 118
parsley, 136
peach, 12, 21, 67, 96, 99, 103, 135, 169, 185
peanut, 78, 144
pear, 12, 21, 57, 67, 70, 72, 77, 80, 85, 99-101, 108, 124, 128, 159, 163-164, 169-170, 184
peat, 6, 16, 18-19, 21-22, 27, 48, 54, 58-62, 93, 100, 120, 122, 162, 185
pecan, 12, 21, 23, 38-39, 44, 67, 76, 91, 101, 108, 115, 165, 185
pepper, 23, 67, 72, 78, 84, 88, 101, 107-108, 111, 114-115, 117, 122, 129-131, 134, 136, 138, 144, 149-150
peppercorn, 103, 105, 110, 114, 117
peppermint, 13, 22, 38, 101, 139, 145
peppers, 68, 78, 117, 121, 139
perfume, 134, 148
persimmon, 12, 21, 102
phenol, 48, 54, 60, 67, 70, 75, 77, 81, 83, 85, 93, 98, 100-101, 128-130, 132, 138, 146
pickleback, 133
pilsner, 176, 179
pimento, 12, 21, 86, 104, 185

pineapple, 69, 72, 77-78, 82, 86, 91, 104, 117, 119, 121-122, 136, 139, 181
pinenut, 106
pistachios, 51
plantain, 152
plum, 12, 21, 67, 96, 99, 103-105, 135, 185
pomegranate, 77
poplar, 79
poppy, 78
potatoes, 85
potpourri, 83, 152
prune, 83, 103, 119
psidium, 82
puama, 13, 22, 121, 163-164
pumice, 125

Q

quassia, 13, 22, 123, 163, 169
quercus, 23, 104-107

R

raisin, 52, 72, 75, 79, 94, 103-104, 106, 110, 150-151
raspberry, 110, 128
rauchbier, 28, 45, 54, 72
rauchmalt, 27, 54
rose, 83, 135, 152, 177
rosemary, 97, 114, 149
rotisserie, 45
rum, 14, 18, 20, 36, 47, 51, 94, 98, 107, 151, 165
rye, 14-15, 18, 50-53, 165, 189

S

sage, 13, 22, 93, 97, 123, 125, 130, 142-143, 145-147, 155, 161, 163, 168, 184
sagebrush, 155

salicin, 124
sandalwood, 114, 138, 142
sassafras, 12, 15, 21, 105
sawdust, 44
schlenkerla, 28, 35
sherry, 90-91, 117, 131, 134
shochu, 51
skullcap, 13, 22, 148-149, 163
spearmint, 13, 22, 38, 139, 145, 149
strawberries, 80, 83, 96
sulfur, 26, 36, 70-71, 79, 108-109, 111, 114, 133, 161, 184
sylvestris, 80

T

tabasco, 12, 23, 107, 111, 117
tails, 47
tannins, 105
tarragon, 13, 22, 88, 136, 151
thyme, 102, 114, 121, 145, 151
tincture, 113, 125
tobacco, 22, 47, 68, 77, 84, 98, 108, 112, 125
tonic, 150
triticale, 50-55, 189
tritordeum, 52

V

vanilla, 71, 73, 81-82, 84, 90, 92, 98, 104-106, 110-111, 124-125, 138, 180
vermouth, 155

W

walnut, 12, 21, 70, 75, 77, 89, 101, 103, 106, 116, 125, 168-170, 184
wax, 93, 109, 122
weyermann, 46, 54
wormwood, 13, 22, 113, 155, 189

Y

yohimbe, 13, 22, 125

List of scientific names of plant species in this book

Species	scientific name	Species	scientific name
alder	Alnus tenuifolia	sassafras	Sassafras albidum
almond	Prunus dulcis	white oak	quercus alba
apple	Malus domestica	bayberry root	Myrica cerifera
apricot	Prunus armeniaca	birch bark	Betula papyrifera
ash	Fraxinus americana	blackberry root	Rubus armeniacus
avacodo	Persea americana	butternut bark	Juglans cinerea
beechwood	Fagus sylvatica	cascara bark	Rhamnus purshiana
birch	Betula cordifolia	catuaba bark	Trichilia catigua
black walnut	Juglans nigra	fringe tree bark	Chionanthus virginicus
cabernet barrel wood	Quercus alba - white oak	jamaican dogwood bark	Piscidia piscipula
crabapple	Malus sylvestris	muira puama bark	Ptychopetalum olacoides
cherry	Prunus avium	prickly ash bark	Zanthoxylum clava-herculis
cedar	Juniperus virginiana	quassia bark	Quassia amara
grape	Vitis vinifera	white willow bark	Salix alba
Hawaiian Guava	Psidium guajava	barberry root	Berberis vulgaris
Hawaiian Kiawe	Prosopis pallida	yohimbe bark	Corynanthe yohimbe
Hawaiian Ohia	Metrosideros polymorpha	calamus root	Acorus calamus
hickory	Carya ovata	catnip	Nepeta cataria
jamaican pimento wood	Pimenta dioica	clove	Syzygium aromaticum
lemon	Citrus limon	ginger	Zingiber officinale
Lilac	Syringa vulgaris	jasmine	Jasminum sp.
macadamia	Macadamia integrifolia	lavender	Lavandula intermedia
manzanita wood	Arctostaphylos manzanita	lemon balm	Melissa officinalis
maplewood	*Acer saccharum*	licorice	Glycyrrhiza glabra
mesquite	Prosopis alba	mint	Mentha spicata
mulberry	Morus rubra	mugwort	Artemisia vulgaris
nectarine	Prunus persica	osha	Ligusticum porteri
olivewood	Olea europaea	peppermint	Mentha piperita
orange	Citrus sinensis	sage - white, black, and hummingl	Salvia apiana
peach	Prunus persica	sagebrush	Artemisia tridentata
peat	n/a	skullcap	Scutellaria lateriflora
pear	Pyrus communis	spearmint	Mentha spicata
pecan	Carya illinoinensis	sweet cicely	NOT USED
persimmon	Diospyros virginiana	terragon	Artemisia dracunculus
plum	Prunus americana	violet	Viola tricolor
red oak	Quercus rubra	wormwood	Artemisia absinthium
		yerba buena	Clinopodium douglasii

Fire Water © 2013 by Darek Bell

Photo copyrights:
Shutterstock copyrights:
95, "mesquite tree beans" © Shutterstock/ Rodney Mehring.
104, "Persimmon." © Shutterstock/Yuryzap.
84, "Cedar Tree," © Shutterstock/Skowron.
8, "Raw split cedar wood logs cut to length in a lumber storage yard - Western Oregon. old growth salvaged timber stacked and ready to be sawn into shakes and shingles for use in building construction" © Shutterstock/M. Niebuhr.
8, "A crabapple tree in full bloom against a blue sky and green grass." © Shutterstock/Michael Shake.
8, "Gorgeous early spring blooming cherry trees in pink and white." © Shutterstock/Hannamariah.
8, "Ripening cherries on orchard tree." © Shutterstock/Evoken.
8, "Wine Barrels" © Shutterstock/Neale Cousland.
8, "Walnut tree orchard" © Shutterstock/Mike Neale.
8, "Walnuts keep up on a tree" © Shutterstock/Nataly Lukhanina.
8, "birch wood" © Shutterstock/kzww.
8, "Pile of birch wood" © Shutterstock/CCat82.
8, "Sawn beech logs on grass" © Shutterstock/Catalin Petolea.
8, "Looking to the misty trees beech forest" © Shutterstock/Pady.
8, "Golden ash tree in autumn" © Shutterstock/metalstock.
8, "Avacodo tree" © Shutterstock/CarlaVanWagoner.
8, "Ripe tasty apricot on tree" © Shutterstock/saiko3p.
8, "Trees with red apples in an orchard" © Shutterstock/Catalin Petolea.
8, "a field of blossoming almond trees in full bloom" © Shutterstock/Sarra2.
8, "alder firewood" © Shutterstock/nito.
8, "Red grapes in the vineyard" © Shutterstock/Alex Moe.
8, "fire and smoke isolated on black" © Shutterstock/PeterPhoto123.
8, "guava fruit on the tree," © Shutterstock/Skowron.
8, "Tall Old Hickory Tree," © Shutterstock/Cynthia Burkhardt.
8, "Lemon tree," © Shutterstock/ODM.
8, "Flowering Lilac Tree. The Genus is Most Closely Related to Ligustrum (Privet), Classified with it in Oleaceae Tribus Oleeae Subtribus Ligustrinae," © Shutterstock/welcomia.
8, "bunch of violet lilac flower (shallow DOF)," © Shutterstock/KULISH VIKTORIIA.
8, "macadamia nuts hanging on tree," © Shutterstock/joloei.
1, "Heap of spelt, isolated on white," © Shutterstock/Jessmine,
2, "Oat flakes closeup," © Shutterstock/Subbotina Anna,
3, "Quinoa grain in glass bowl on white background," © Shutterstock/Elena Elisseeva,
4, "a small bag of buckwheat on white background," © Shutterstock/buiry,
5, "Maturing millet," © Shutterstock/huyangshu,
6, "millet. background of ripe grain.," © Olena Pivnenko,
7, "Closeup on pile of organic whole grain wheat kernels and ears," © Shutterstock/Elena Elisseeva,
8, "Mature Sorghum," © Shutterstock/Lemon Man,
82, "A crabapple tree in full bloom against a blue sky and green grass," © Shutterstock/Michael Shake,
107, "sassafras plant," © Shutterstock/Roger Dale Pleis,
62, "kilns, the pagoda-roof of the peat-fire in a scottish Whisky-distillery," © Shutterstock/Klaus Rainer Krieger,
73, "Avacodo tree," © Shutterstock/CarlaVanWagoner,
61, "peat mining on Islay today is practiced for the Whisky-industry, rarely for heating.," © Shutterstock/Klaus Rainer Krieger,
98, "Nectarine orchard," © Shutterstock/Hannamariah,
98, "Nectarines on the tree," © Shutterstock/Hannamariah,
87, "Tall Old Hickory Tree," © Shutterstock/Cynthia Burkhardt,
103, "pecan on a tree," © Shutterstock/Mike Donenfeld,
78, "Walnut tree orchard," © Shutterstock/,
97, "golf cart in front of a crepe myrtle tree," © Shutterstock/William J. Mahnken,
95, "Mesquite trees in a park at sunset useful as background© Shutterstock/Chris Curtis,
95, "Mesquite chips add flavor to barbecue or barbeque," © Shutterstock/C. Kurt Holter,
100, "Orange tree in Andalusia, Sevilla, Spain," © Shutterstock/Luca Grandinetti,
98, "Flowering mulberry tree - the Latin name is Morus Nigra - on its natural background," © Shutterstock/Katalin Kiszály,
72, "Ash tree," © Shutterstock/Pefkos,
99, "Detail of olive tree branch," © Shutterstock/Tomo Jesenicnik,
108, "A large old Oak Tree with beautiful blue sky with clouds in the background, horizontal with copy space," © Shutterstock/Cheryl E. Davis,
68, "alder firewood," © Shutterstock/Alex Moe,
62, "Peat drying oven in Islay distillery," © Shutterstock/Jaime Pharr,
104, "Persimmon tree with mature orange fruits, Tuscany (and small willow-leafed pear)," © Shutterstock/Malgorzata Kistryn,
80, "Gorgeous early spring blooming cherry trees in pink and white..," © Shutterstock/Hannamariah,
100, "Orange tree full of oranges," © Shutterstock/N/A,
69, "a field of blossoming almond trees in full bloom," © Shutterstock/N/A,
66, "Sawmill (lumber mill)," © Shutterstock/N/A,
105, "plum tree," © Shutterstock/ N/A,
72, "Ash Tree Flowers - Fraxinus excelsior," © Shutterstock/Martin Fowler,
80, "Cherry tree dried wood trunks for firewood laying on brown floor," © Shutterstock/ holbox,

Your secret weapon in the fight against average whiskeys!

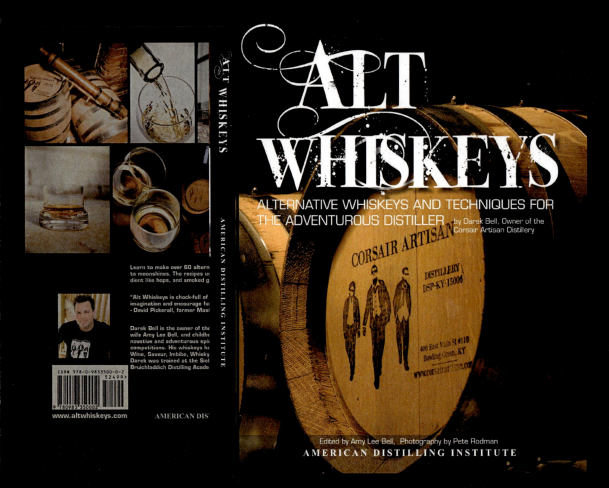

ALSO BY DAREK BELL

"Alt Whiskeys is a turning point in the literature of American distilling. There's nothing else out there that captures, page after page, our modern distillers' spirit of innovation with new ingredients, techniques, and equipment"
–Matthew Rowley

AVAILABLE NOW AT
ALTWHISKEYS.COM

SMOKED WHISKEY TASTING KIT!

Own a part of the smoked whiskey library from this book to make your own incredibly complex smoked whiskeys. A set of 24 unique smoke flavors pulled from the hardwoods, herbs, and bark smoke sources that made the individual smoked whiskeys in this book.

Very limited supply.

Will you use it for Good…Or Evil?

AVAILABLE NOW AT
ALTWHISKEYS.COM

sourcing smoked malts

North American Craft Maltsters	phone	location	website
Academy Malt Co.		Indianapolis, Indiana	
Blacklands Malt	512-944-3259	Austin, Texas	http://www.blacklandsmalt.com/
California Craft Malt Co.	n/a	Oakland, California	n/a
California Malting Co.	805-325-9020	Santa Barbara, California	n/a
Christensen Farms Malting Co.	503-550-3576	McMinnville, Oregon	www.HeritageMalt.com
Colorado Malting Co.	719-580-5084	Alamosa, Colorado	http://www.coloradomaltingcompany.com/
Copper Fox Distillery	(540) 987-8554	Sperryville, Virginia	copperfox.biz
Corsair Artisan Distillery	615-351-9442	Nashville, Tennessee	http://www.corsairartisan.com/
Deer Creek Malthouse	717-746-6258	Philadelphia, Pennsylvania	deercrekmalt.com
Doehnel Floor Malting	360-982-1395	Victoria, BC, Canada	n/a
Farm Boy Farms	919-696-7850	Pittsboro, North Carolina	farmboybrewery.com
Farmhouse Malt NYC	607-227-0638	Newark Valley, New York	farmhousemalt.com
Gold Rush Malt LLC	n/a	n/a	www.goldrushmalt.com/
Grouse Malting & Roasting Co.	419-606-1852	Nunn, Colorado	http://www.grouseco.com/
High Desert Malt	n/a	n/a	n/a
Hillrock Estate Distillery	518-329-1023	Ancram, New York	http://hillrockdistillery.com/
Maine Craft Distilling	(207) 798-2528	Portland, ME	www.mainecraftdistilling.com
Maltarie Frontenac Inc.	418-338-9563	Quebec, Canada	www.MalterieFrontenac.com
Mammoth Malt	(217) 387-2451	Thawville, Illinois	
Mecca Grade Growers LLC	541-231-2801	Madras, OR	
Michigan Malt	989-954-5962	Shepherd, Michigan	http://www.michiganmalt.com/
New York Craft Malt	585-813-5389	Batavia, New York	http://www.newyorkcraftmalt.com/
Niagara Malt	716-861-9887	Cambria, NY	http://www.niagaramalt.com/
Our Mutual Friend Malt & Brew	951-265-4192	Denver, Colorado	
Owens Malt		Hayward, California	
Peterson Quality Malt	802-989-0014	Monkton, Vermont	qualitymalt@gmail.com
Pioneer Malting	n/a	n/a	n/a
Pilot Malt House	616-209-8388	Jenison, Michigan	
Rebel Malting Co.	775-997-6411	Reno, Nevada	www.RebelMalting.com
Riverbend Malt House	828-450-1081	Asheville, North Carolina	www.RiverBendMalt.com
Rocky Mountain Distilling	970-306-7766		
Rogue Ales Farmstead Malthouse		Newport, Oregon	http://rogue.com/
Skagit Valley Malting	360-982-1395	Mt Vernon, WA	www.skagitvalleymalting.com/
Slow Hand Malting	802-846-7681	Hinesburg, VT	slowhandmalting.com
Valley Malt	413-349-9098	Hadley, Massachusetts	valleymalt.com
Large Maltsters			
Briess Malt & Ingredients Co.	800-657-0806	Chilton, WI	http://www.briess.com/
Weyermann¨ Specialty Malting Co.	+ 49 (0)951 93 220-0	Bamberg, Germany	http://www.weyermann.de/
Simpsons Malt	+44 (0)1289 330033	Northumberland, UK	http://www.simpsonsmalt.co.uk/

Made in the USA
San Bernardino, CA
11 March 2019